How To
Use Tarot Spreads

Llewellyn Publications
Woodbury, Minnesota

How To Use Tarot Spreads © 1997 and 2006 by Sylvia Abraham. All rights reserved. No part of this book may be used or reproduced in any manner whatsoever, including Internet usage, without written permission from Llewellyn Publications, except in the case of brief quotations embodied in critical articles and reviews.

REVISED EDITION
First printing, 2006

First edition, seven printings

Book design by Donna Burch
Cards on cover from the *Universal Tarot* by Roberto de Angelis, reprinted with permission from Lo Scarabeo
Cover design by Gavin Dayton Duffy
Editing by Lee Lewis
Interior art by Llewellyn art department

Llewellyn is a registered trademark of Llewellyn Worldwide, Ltd.

Library of Congress Cataloging-in-Publication Data
Abraham, Sylvia, 1924–
   How to use tarot spreads / Sylvia Abraham. — 2nd ed.
      p.   cm. — (How to series)
   Includes bibliographical references.
   ISBN 0-7387-0816-X
   1. Tarot. 2. Fortune-telling by cards. I. Title. II. Llewellyn's how to series.
   BF1879.T2A38 2006
   133.3'2424—dc22
                                                    2005044327

ISBN 13: 978-0-7387-0816-4
ISBN 10: 0-7387-0816-X

Llewellyn Worldwide does not participate in, endorse, or have any authority or responsibility concerning private business transactions between our authors and the public.

   All mail addressed to the author is forwarded but the publisher cannot, unless specifically instructed by the author, give out an address or phone number.

   Any Internet references contained in this work are current at publication time, but the publisher cannot guarantee that a specific location will continue to be maintained. Please refer to the publisher's website for links to authors' websites and other sources.

Llewellyn Publications
A Division of Llewellyn Worldwide, Ltd.
2143 Wooddale Drive, Dept. 0-7387-0816-X
Woodbury, MN 55125-2989, U.S.A.
www.llewellyn.com

Printed in the United States of America

Contents

Acknowledgments

After writing my first book, *How to Read the Tarot*, a friend suggested I write a book on tarot spreads. Busy with other projects at the time, I put that idea on the back burner. Suddenly, during the early months of 1995, I found myself involved with writing this book on tarot spreads! When the time is right, everything falls into place, or so it seems to me.

I want to thank Lynnette for her persistence and her help, and Cathy, who gave me a different slant on several of the spreads. My thanks to Gilbert and Phillip for their input, and all my other students who participated in this endeavor. I also wish to thank my daughter Lee for her artistic help with the spreads. Several of the spreads concerned family members whom I coaxed into sitting for a reading.

For all tarot readers who may need new ideas about spreads, I hope this book will be helpful. For new tarot readers who would like to understand how to read the tarot, I hope this book fills their needs as well.

Sylvia Abraham

One

Introduction to Tarot

There has been much information and conjecture on the beginnings of tarot, but no conclusive proof of its origins. Many people believe that tarot was discovered in the fourteenth century and have woven stories around this idea in order to support their premise. One thing is for sure—the tarot works! The cards have been used for centuries and that is proof enough of their authenticity.

As a beginner, the more books you read about tarot, the more confident you will become. The tarot cards are ideal tools for meditation, and by working with the cards in this way you will discover further information about them that you will not find in books.

The following pages provide thumbnail sketches of the upright and reversed meanings of each card based on a system I developed in my book *How to Read the Tarot*. Some readers prefer to use only the upright meanings of cards in their readings. If it works, great! If you wish to use reversed cards in your reading, cut your deck into two parts, turn one in the opposite direction, and shuffle the cards together. Have faith—the cards work no matter if read as upright or reversed. Enjoy the spreads and be sure to try the Magical Lottery spread in the last chapter. Who knows, you could win!

Preparing a Reading

Reading tarot spreads is easy. Follow the steps outlined below for a positive tarot reading:

- Select a spread that best fits the circumstances the querent (the person for whom you are reading) would like to examine in the reading.

- Have the querent shuffle the deck of tarot cards. Ask him or her to make a wish and concentrate on his or her question. If desired, the querent can cut the cards.

- Have the querent hand the cards back to you.

- Lay out the cards according to the format of the selected spread.

- Look over the spread and check for repeated elements:

  How many wands appear?
  How many cups?
  How many pentacles?
  How many swords?

- Check the number of each card and notice if any are repeated.

- Are there many major arcana or court cards? If there are, then too many people are involved in the querent's life.

- Read the cards according to your preference, either upright or reversed.

- Be as truthful as possible, but always try to end the reading on a positive note.

- Do not read too many spreads for the same person on a single day—it will create confusion in that person's mind. Tell this individual that he or she must wait a week before you read for him or her again.

Note: If any cards fall out of the deck during shuffling, be sure to incorporate those into your reading as well. All of these cards have information concerning the querent. Check the bottom card of the deck after you have laid out the spread; there is a message there as well.

Beginning tarot readers: Read through this book first and then try your skill at reading the spreads. Experience is the best teacher and reading for others hones your talents and enhances your intuition. Trust yourself always.

The reader has an obligation to the client that must not be taken lightly. Be responsible with the information and be blessed.

The Tarot

Major and Minor Arcana

The Fool 0

Key word: EVERYONE

Upright: I desire new experiences and adventures. Indicates a need for caution. Watch your footing.

Reversed: Lacking confidence. Take responsibility for one's actions. Curb anxiety, release fears.

The Magician I

Key words: I WILL

Upright: I will have new beginnings in many directions. Leadership potential. New growth.

Reversed: I will not have new beginnings at this time. Lack of ambition or drive. Strong sexual focus.

The four aces have the same key words as THE MAGICIAN: I WILL.

Ace of Wands

Upright: I will have new beginnings in my work and social life. New opportunities. A birth.

Reversed: I will not have new beginnings in my work or social life. Trips deferred. Plans canceled.

Ace of Cups

Upright: I will have new beginnings in love relationships. New residence. Happiness. Emotionally upbeat. Peace and good health.

Reversed: I will not have new beginnings in love. Emotional instability. Loss. Separation.

Ace of Pentacles
Upright: I will have new beginnings with money. Prosperity. Inheritance. Raise in pay.
Reversed: I will not have new beginnings with money. Financial picture gloomy. Greed. Jealousy.

Ace of Swords
Upright: I will have new beginnings in problems and troubles. Loss. Potential for operation.
Reversed: I will not have new beginnings in problems and troubles. Remove old ideas. Be confident.

The High Priestess II
Key words: I KNOW
Upright: I know about the world and its duality. Memory, reason, secrets, and the subconscious.
Reversed: I don't know about the world. Closed-minded. Unskilled. Selfish, fearful, and egotistical.

The four twos have the same key words as THE HIGH PRIESTESS: I KNOW.

Two of Wands
Upright: I know my work and social activities. Having the world in one's hand. Success in business. Confidence.
Reversed: I don't know my work or place in society. Unbalanced actions, fear of failure. Lacking skills.

Two of Cups
Upright: I know about love and emotions. A good relationship is emotionally healthy. Birth. Happy events.

Reversed: I know nothing about love. Unhappy emotions. Sexual problems. Loss or separation. Health issues.

Two of Pentacles

Upright: I know how to balance my money. Financial gain. Budgets work. Prosperity-minded. Good health.
Reversed: I don't know how to handle money. Spendthrift. Depression over finances. Poverty-minded.

Two of Swords

Upright: I know my problems and troubles and don't wish to see them. Fear of being hurt. Unclear thinking.
Reversed: I don't know my problems and troubles and don't want to see them. Illusory thinking. Fear of new knowledge.

The Empress III

Key words: I MAKE
Upright: I make my experiences. I create my happiness, my enjoyment, and my life. Potential for pregnancy. Could represent one's mother or an older female.
Reversed: I don't make myself happy. I don't use my creative talents. Problems with one's mother or other females. No pregnancy. Lacking confidence.

The four threes have the same key words as THE EMPRESS: I MAKE.

Three of Wands

Upright: I make my work and social life. Creatively visualizing new work and good times.

Reversed: I don't make my work or social activities. Lacking faith in personal abilities. Unhappiness.

Three of Cups

Upright: I make myself happy doing what I like. Good times with friends. Pregnancy. Marriage.
Reversed: I don't make myself happy in love. An emotional drain. Miscarriage. Alcohol or drug problems. Loneliness.

Three of Pentacles

Upright: I make my money. I am a master craftsman. Creative talents bring financial rewards.
Reversed: I don't make money. Overqualified or underpaid at one's job. Health or money problems.

Three of Swords

Upright: I make my problems and troubles. A love triangle. Shedding tears. Separation or divorce.
Reversed: I don't make my problems or troubles. Rival. Feeling stabbed in the back. Deceit.

The Emperor IV

Key words: I REALIZE
Upright: I realize I am the boss, leader, and initiator. I am original. I am a father figure. Action, balance, stability, and power.
Reversed: I don't realize who I am. Lacking authority. Immature. Inexperienced and unstable.

The four fours have the same key words as THE EMPEROR: I REALIZE.

Four of Wands

Upright: I realize my work and social activities. Balanced work and home situations. Marriage.
Reversed: I do not realize imbalances in my home or work environment. Lack of prosperity. Not a fruitful time.

Four of Cups

Upright: I realize my past love and emotional experiences. Old habit patterns are holding me back from being involved with new relationships.
Reversed: I do not realize my emotions are being drained. Disappointed in love. Feeling rejected. Some loss. Broken relationship.

Four of Pentacles

Upright: I realize the value of money. Avarice. Selling property. Faith in material possessions.
Reversed: I do not realize the value of money. Spend-thrift. Gambling. A need to balance the budget.

Four of Swords

Upright: I realize my problems and troubles. Rest from strife. Need faith to overcome struggles.
Reversed: I don't realize my problems and troubles. Burning the candle at both ends. Health issues.

The Hierophant V

Key words: I BELIEVE
Upright: I believe in my inner teacher or higher self. Resentment of authority or control by others. Need to meditate. Inner guidance.

Reversed: I do not believe in an inner teacher. Indulgent, pleasure-seeking, and materialistic.

The four fives have the same key words as THE HIERO-PHANT: I BELIEVE.

Five of Wands
Upright: I believe in work and social activities. I believe in my ideas, will, and ego.
Reversed: I don't believe in my work or society. Disharmony. Little faith in one's own abilities or ego.

Five of Cups
Upright: I believe in love but have a fear of commitment. Crying over spilled milk. Broken romance.
Reversed: I don't believe in love or romance. An emotional crisis. Divorce or separation. Death.

Five of Pentacles
Upright: I believe in money; it is my god. Unemployment. Crippling ideas. Drugs. Poverty-minded.
Reversed: I don't believe that money is my god. A new job or work that is more difficult. Seek your inner guide.

Five of Swords
Upright: I believe in problems and troubles for myself or others. Empty victory. Loss of friends through cruelty.
Reversed: I don't believe in problems or troubles for myself or others. Seeking mental balance.

The Lovers VI

Key words: I CHOOSE
Upright: I choose my life. Seeking answers from a higher self. Knowing the positive and the negative in life. A trip or social event.
Reversed: Other people make my choices. Engagement or marriage plans delayed. Little trust in self.

The four sixes have the same key words as THE LOVERS: I CHOOSE.

Six of Wands

Upright: I choose my work and social activities. Victory! Right use of ego and will.
Reversed: I don't make choices at work or socially. Temptations overcome common sense. Delays.

Six of Cups

Upright: I make choices in my love relationships. I choose to control my emotions. Potential to live in the past, or someone from the past returns. New love affair or marriage.
Reversed: Others make decisions for me. An emotionally draining situation. Loss. Divorce. Health problems.

Six of Pentacles

Upright: I make choices with my money. Desire to be fair and share resources. Helping others.
Reversed: I don't make choices with my money. Poverty-minded. Not charitable. Health matters.

Six of Swords

Upright: I choose my problems and troubles. I am tempted to run away rather than face my problems.
Reversed: I have no choice to make about my problems and troubles. I must stay and face the situation. No trips at this time.

The Chariot VII

Key words: THE PATH
Upright: My mental path will take me to victory. I control my senses through my mind. I trust my higher self.
Reversed: My mental path is unwise. Focus is on the material aspect, not mental. Self-indulgence. Opinionated.

The four sevens have the same key words as THE CHARIOT: THE PATH.

Seven of Wands

Upright: I take the mental path in my work and social life. Success and victory in business. Feeling superior at work. New ideas. Loner.
Reversed: The wrong path leads to defeat at work or socially. Feeling inferior or incompetent. Material desires. Drugs.

Seven of Cups

Upright: The path leads to success in love. Mental control over emotions, use of creative visualization. Retreat into alcohol or drugs.
Reversed: The path leads to defeat in love and emotional needs. Loss or separation. Little trust or faith in self.

Seven of Pentacles

Upright: The path leads to money and success. Financial responsibilities. Prosperity-minded. Confidence.
Reversed: The path to money is uncertain. Poverty-minded. Little money sense. Health affected by negativity.

Seven of Swords

Upright: The path leads to problems and troubles. Temporary situation. Feeling cheated or some loss.
Reversed: Lack of mental clarity leads to the path of problems and troubles. Jealousy. Unhappy relationship. Situation is not over at this time.

Strength VIII

Key word: STRENGTH
Upright: Having the strength to overcome any difficulties. Courage and endurance. Creative. Control over desires.
Reversed: Lacking strength. Little self-control. Egotistical and vain. Not trustworthy. Shallow.

The four eights have the same keyword as STRENGTH: STRENGTH.

Eight of Wands

Upright: I have the strength to do my work and be involved in my social life. Messages regarding work. Travel for work or pleasure.
Reversed: Lacking strength in work or social activities. Delays and frustrations. No travel plans.

Eight of Cups
Upright: I have strength in my love and emotions. A search for spiritual values. Turning one's back on temptations. Letting go of past experiences.
Reversed: Lacking strength in love and emotions. Emotional drain due to loss, separation, or divorce.

Eight of Pentacles
Upright: Having the strength to make money. Learning new skills. Gaining confidence.
Reversed: Not having the strength to work for one's money. Desire for quick, easy money. Criminal activities. Dislike of hard work.

Eight of Swords
Upright: Having the strength to cope with problems and troubles. Feeling in bondage. On unsafe ground. Potential for health problems.
Reversed: Lack of strength in handling troubles or problems. Feeling unsafe in the midst of chaos. Let go of unhealthy situations now.

The Hermit IX
Key words: WISDOM THROUGH EXPERIENCE
Upright: Using the wisdom of one's experiences in positive ways. New lessons in one's life. Meetings with an older person. One's inner teacher.
Reversed: Lack of wisdom gained through experiences. Selfish and intolerant. Sexual inhibitions. Fear.

The four nines have the same key words as THE HERMIT: WISDOM THROUGH EXPERIENCE.

Nine of Wands

Upright: Using wisdom at work and socially. Ability to protect oneself in business or relationships. Using fair tactics at work.

Reversed: Lack of wisdom at work or socially. Open to abuse from outside sources.

Nine of Cups

Upright: The wish card! If upright, you get your wish. Wisdom gained through experience in love and emotions.

Reversed: You don't get your wish at this time. Emotional drain. Lacking wisdom. Loss or separation.

Nine of Pentacles

Upright: Using wisdom in financial matters. Independence. Inheritance. Healthy existence.

Reversed: Not using wisdom in financial matters. Dependency brings depression. Spendthrift.

Nine of Swords

Upright: Experiences with problems and troubles bring wisdom. Despair. A crisis period. Loss. Illness.

Reversed: Experiences have not brought wisdom or understanding. Problems and troubles can worsen. Little confidence. Have faith.

The Wheel of Fortune X

Key words: CHANGES AND NEW CYCLES

Upright: Time to make changes, take a gamble, or make plans to travel. Potential for marriage.
Reversed: Changes are not likely now. Cycle not finished. Take care of health and diet.

The four tens have the same key words as THE WHEEL OF FORTUNE: CHANGES AND NEW CYCLES.

Ten of Wands

Upright: Major changes at work or socially. Laying down burdens. New business methods. Travel.
Reversed: No changes at this time. Don't gamble. Obstacles are frustrating. Back problems.

Ten of Cups

Upright: Changes in love and emotions. New cycle in family relations. A move or short trip.
Reversed: An emotional drain through family affairs. Overindulgence results in ill health. Loss, separation, or divorce. Unhappiness.

Ten of Pentacles

Upright: Major changes in finances. New home, job, or inheritance. Success in money matters.
Reversed: No changes in finances. Misfortune with money. Older people may be a burden.

Ten of Swords

Upright: Major changes in problems and troubles. Burdens may be removed. Cycle of negativity may be ending. Back problems are relieved.

Reversed: No changes in problems and troubles. Need to have courage to face difficulties. Situation not as negative as it seems.

Justice XI

Key words: JUSTICE, EQUILIBRIUM

Upright: Balance, law, harmony, karma, and fairness. Seeking justice in business or personally. A successful legal battle. Potential marriage.

Reversed: Legal complications due to anger and hostilities. Prejudiced views. Overconfidence can lead to failure. Depression. Health affected.

The Hanged Man XII

Key words: SACRIFICE, REVERSAL

Upright: Feeling sacrificed to the will and desires of others. In bondage to personal views. Duty to family. Maintain one's perspective. Meditate.

Reversed: Procrastination. Fooled by others. Little or no trust in a higher power. Drugs or alcohol used to escape. Illusionary.

Death XIII

Key word: TRANSFORMATION

Upright: End of a situation. Change for the better. New ideas and future plans are healthy. Money comes to you. Be open to love. Enlightenment.

Reversed: Stagnation, frustration, and unhappiness. No transformation. Lost love. Jealousy, anger, and resentment can affect health.

Temperance XIV

Key word: MODERATION

Upright: Positive use of energy, self-control, and harmony. Trusting the inner self for guidance. Patience during difficult experiences. Meditate.

Reversed: Self-indulgent, restless, with little control over emotions. Negative use of sexual energy. Ignorance of higher laws. Having little faith.

The Devil XV

Key words: MATERIALISM, DECEPTION

Upright: Bound to the world by physical and material greed. Desire for social success. Acceptance at any cost. Creative energy wasted in pleasure-seeking.

Reversed: Desire to lift the veil of illusion. Accepting responsibility for one's actions. Change diet for better health.

The Tower XVI

Key word: CATASTROPHE

Upright: Doing away with old habit patterns. Overthrow of false ideas. Strife and discord in relationships. Unexpected events. Risk of accidents.

Reversed: Refusing to change old habit patterns. Sexual needs, resentment, and jealousy cause catastrophes.

The Star XVII

Key words: DISCOVERY, ASPIRATION

Upright: Faith and trust in life. Setting new goals. New opportunities. Optimistic. Using skills.

Reversed: Pessimistic regarding career moves, relationships, and life in general. Not setting new goals for the future. Health matters. Low self-esteem.

The Moon XVIII

Key words: ATTAINMENT, DECEPTION

Upright: Deception and illusion regarding personal attainment or emotional matters. Overcoming fears from subconscious memories. Psychic ability. A slow but steady climb to enlightenment. Feeling victimized by others.

Reversed: Not seeing or hearing truth. Unconscious actions. Depression due to delayed plans. Feeling betrayed.

The Sun XIX

Key word: RENEWAL

Upright: Seeking truth and happiness. Self-confidence, optimism, and courage. New work in science or mathematics. Open to new thought.

Reversed: Lacking courage or confidence. Dishonesty creates discord. Sexual needs create problems. Loss of trust from others. Ostentatiousness.

Judgement XX

Key word: AWARENESS

Upright: Change of residence, new position or career. Faith in a higher power. New knowledge brings joy and happiness. Not accepting traditional views. Health improves.

Reversed: Materialistic approach to life. Blind faith and mistaken judgment. Loss or separation from family. Health matters arise.

The World XXI
Key words: COSMIC CONSCIOUSNESS
Upright: Success in all endeavors. A new career or move. Goals attained. Long journey proves beneficial. Feeling supported by inner resources. Victory. Balance.
Reversed: No success or material gain. Plans delayed or defeated. Lacking vision or truth. Fear of change or the unknown. Little mental growth.

Court Cards

There are sixteen court cards. These cards refer to people in one's life and can indicate a love interest, family members, people at work, or relatives. They can indicate a certain person coming into or leaving the querent's life, and they may also indicate "ideas" that are in one's thoughts. If the last card in a spread is a court card, it can mean that someone other than the querent must make the final decision on the issue in question.

Kings

Kings signify a father figure—authority, wisdom, and experience. Males age thirty-five or older.

Queens

Queens signify a mother image. She is an authority figure and indicates maturity, nurturing, and understanding. Females age thirty-five or older.

Note: If a King or Queen is reversed in a spread, the card may represent a negative person. Also, the King reversed may indicate a female of that card's corresponding astrological sign (positive or negative). The Queen reversed may indicate a male of that card's astrological sign (positive or negative).

Knights

Knights are messengers. When the card is upright, it refers to a male or a positive message. (The Knight of Swords upright is the exception—the message is not usually pleasant.) This card reversed will indicate a female of the corresponding astrological sign. Persons age twenty-five to forty.

Pages

Pages represent children or young people in various stages of growth and inexperience. They can also indicate messages or symbolize some types of problems. At times, a Page upright can denote a male and, reversed, a female. The Page can also represent a feminine male child or a strong female child. The Pages can be deceptive! Persons age one to twenty-five.

Divinatory Meanings
King of Wands

Upright: This King is independent, influential, and an authority figure. He is ambitious, with executive talents and leadership qualities. He has good ideas. He is an Aries type.
Reversed: This King is childish, dependent, and has antisocial attitudes. He can be selfish and domineering—a petty tyrant.

King of Cups

Upright: This King is emotional, loving, caring, and nurturing. A good family man. He needs to feel safe and secure in his professional and personal life. He is a Cancer type.

Reversed: This King is cold, uncaring, and not nurturing. He can be untrustworthy in business or relationships. Potential to be ruthless and calculating.

King of Pentacles

Upright: The King of Pentacles is a good financial adviser—practical and reliable. He is slow to anger but can be very stubborn. Good in business, banking, and sales. He is a Taurus type.

Reversed: This King is selfish, lazy, impractical, and a speculator. He loves luxury, is sensual, and desires pleasure. He can be dishonest, with questionable judgment.

King of Swords

Upright: This King is a professional man, a lawyer, or in the military. He has mental dexterity and is a good counselor with lots of nervous energy. He is a Gemini type. This card can also indicate the querent's need for a lawyer.

Reversed: This King is fickle and superficial. He dissipates his energy and rebels against authority. He is unkind, a gossip, and unstable. Potential loss in a lawsuit.

Queen of Wands

Upright: This Queen desires success in work and in her social life. She is an authority figure—ambitious and ego-driven, needing admiration and attention. She is a Leo type.

Reversed: This Queen is domineering, demanding, and controlling at work and in social situations. She is unloving, lacks humor, and has a large ego. She can be resentful, angry, jealous—even ruthless.

Queen of Cups

Upright: This Queen speaks of love and emotional needs. She is a good wife and mother, and is very protective of her family. Sex is important to her well-being. She is intuitive, intense, and powerful. She is a Scorpio type.

Reversed: This Queen is dishonest in love. Her emotions are drained due to a loss, separation, or other negative event. She has a terrible temper, likes intrigue, and can be jealous of others. Potential to be unfaithful.

Queen of Pentacles

Upright: Making money is the focus for this Queen. She is an idealist and perfectionist, with critical views. She is a Virgo type. This card also represents harvest time after much labor, potential for pregnancy, or gifts from family.

Reversed: This Queen is a spendthrift and lazy. She is a superficial friend, lacks confidence, and is judgmental. She feels imperfect and limits her prosperity. Too much focus on the physical and material.

Queen of Swords

Upright: This Queen often represents a divorced woman or a widow, someone focused on her problems and troubles.

She is strong-willed, sharp-tongued, and temperamental. She desires a relationship and must make decisions. Legal problems may confront her. She is a Libra type.

Reversed: This Queen has problems and troubles but does not wish to see them. She fears divorce or separation. Her sexual needs drive her to a relationship, but she is not always open or honest.

Knight of Wands

Upright: This messenger brings information regarding work and social activities. Good news concerning one's job, planning a trip, or a change of residence. New interests, glad tidings, time to shine. Leo-type energy.

Reversed: The messenger does not arrive or the news is not positive. Delays cause frustration and depression. Expectations are not fulfilled.

Knight of Cups

Upright: Positive messages regarding love and emotional needs. The Knight brings new information about a birth, invitation to a party or wedding, or travel plans. A loving, sensual, and sexual person. Scorpio-type energy.

Reversed: Messages concerning love did not arrive. Invitations, notices of marriages, or birth announcements were not received. An emotional drain involving relationships, friendships, or family. Some loss or a separation.

Knight of Pentacles

Upright: Messages regarding finances. Good news about an inheritance, real estate, or other valuables. This Knight shows good health and vitality. He enjoys material possessions and sensual pleasures and has many desires. Taurus-type energy. Money used for good times.

Reversed: Messages about money not received or not positive. Lack of financial well-being. Delays. Poverty-minded. Being lazy, indulgent, and oversexed causes negative experiences.

Knight of Swords

Upright: This messenger brings news of problems and troubles; rage, anger, and frustration may be in the message. These messages may relate to the querent personally or others close to him or her. Mental aggression may cause physical problems. Think positively. Aquarius-type energy.

Reversed: Messages concerning invitations, notices of marriage or birth, love, or travel plans did not arrive. This Knight is closed-minded and unreliable, lacking discrimination in dealing with others. Wild accusations. Some loss or a separation. This Knight corresponds to the mental plane and can mean "all talk and no action."

Page of Wands

Upright: This Page is eager to experience work and social life. He or she desires freedom and is headstrong, a wanderer. This Page has great expectations and some luck from the gods. May relate to travel, foreign people, and philosophy. Sagittarius-type energy.

Reversed: This Page can be lazy, immoral, and refuse to work. He or she can be fickle, faithless, cruel, and extravagant. This Page can be a gossip and a betrayer of confidences.

Page of Cups

Upright: This Page corresponds to love and emotions. He or she brings good news concerning love relationships, parties, marriages, and births. A person who is creative, has psychic abilities, and can be a healer. Pisces-type energy.

Reversed: A lack of love and an emotional drain. Unhappy news regarding a relationship. This Page has great expectations, which may not be fulfilled. Potential for emotional abuse. Not using creative talents.

Page of Pentacles

Upright: This Page desires financial security, to pursue a career, become a professional, and make it to the top. He or she is ambitious, materialistic, and traditional. Desire for gain. The card of the scholar. Capricorn-type energy.

Reversed: The messages this Page brings are not positive and can refer to health matters. This Page is not interested in work or school and will not set goals. He or she is lazy, selfish, and greedy, and desires the easy life.

Page of Swords

Upright: This Page corresponds to problems and troubles. He or she desires new and novel experiences, new knowledge, and many friendships. This person is motivated by concern for others, and is extroverted, naive, and unconventional. Aquarius-type energy.

Reversed: Problems and troubles descend on this Page due to his or her lack of attention. He or she is apt to be anxious, introverted, and paranoid. Friendships and relationships may be unimportant to this person.

Additional Information

Following is some additional information concerning correspondences of the tarot cards, which can be helpful in the readings.

The information in the following table can be applied to the last card of the spread, allowing you to tell the querent when an event may take place. A reader should have some idea how long the information given is in effect. Information gained in a typical reading can apply to a month, a year, or a lifetime. The information becomes a part of the querent's thinking and they rarely forget what a reader has told them—positive or negative.

Symbol	Time	Seasons	Element
Wands	weeks	spring	fire
Cups	days	summer	water
Pentacles	years	winter	earth
Swords	months	autumn	air

Astrological Signs

Learning more about the astrological signs can deepen your knowledge regarding the cards. What follows is a simple description of the traits of each sign and their correspondences with the tarot suits.

Zodiac correspondences:

Wands: Aries, Leo, Sagittarius

Cups: Cancer, Scorpio, Pisces

Pentacles: Taurus, Virgo, Capricorn

Swords: Gemini, Libra, Aquarius

Aries

This is a fire sign, which means "action and energy." These people are always on the go. They can be childlike, independent, and courageous, and may have leadership qualities. They insist on making changes.

Taurus

This is an earth sign, which corresponds with materialism, physicality, and inertia. These people can work diligently, earn their daily bread, and enjoy the fruits of their labor. They can also be lazy, stolid, stubborn, and overindulgent.

Gemini

This is an air sign, which relates to the mental plane. These people are thinkers, daydreamers, superficial, and charming. They can be tricksters, not always grounded, and love to chatter about any subject.

Cancer

This is a water sign referring to emotions, intuition, nurturing, sensitivity, and caring. These people are called the mothers of the earth. They enjoy home life, real estate, and security.

Leo

This is a fire sign. These people want the spotlight, applause, and attention. They have great expectations and are often disappointed. This is the sign of the ego and is considered the strongest sign of the zodiac.

Virgo

This is an earth sign—physical, material, and stubborn. These people are the workers of the zodiac. They are critical, judgmental, and perfectionist. They are always looking for flaws at work, and are often disappointed in people. They may also deal with health issues.

Libra

This is an air sign. These people seek equality, justice, friends, and lovers. They are creative and tend to be in love with love. They rarely find what they are seeking because they are not balanced in their own lives. They may not treat others with equality or justice.

Scorpio

This is a water sign—intense, possessive, jealous, sexual, and vengeful. Scorpio people are sensitive and emotional. They enjoy working with other people's money or possessions. These people can be very powerful and will experience transformation during their lifetime.

Sagittarius

This is a fire sign. Sagittarians are all about freedom, traveling the world with a pack on their back, mixing with a variety of people, learning new philosophies, and getting a higher education. They create or adapt their moral code to the moment and rarely stay in relationships for long.

Capricorn

This is an earth sign. Capricorns are noted for their desire to succeed. They want a successful social life and lots of money and material possessions. They are persistent, which adds to their success. Unfortunately, some Capricorns will do most anything to get ahead, legal or otherwise.

Aquarius

This is an air sign—brotherhood, friends, hopes, and wishes. These people are inventive, usually positive, and desire to be of service and help humanity. The Aquarian age is upon us and we hope it will bring peace and brotherly love into every heart.

Pisces

This is a water sign—emotional, sensitive, creative, and very psychic. These people have many outlets for their talents, such as being a healer, an artist, or holding a religious position. They have a tendency toward being the victim/martyr.

Two

Love and Romance

The spreads in this chapter all concern love and romance. Everyone is interested in new relationships, romantic involvements, and commitments of some sort. There is much excitement at the prospect of meeting someone new!

The spreads in this chapter are:

A New Lover

A Romantic Attraction

Lovers

Magical Love

Guide for Lovers

All the spreads have readings that explain them, except for the last: Guide for Lovers. Test your own abilities on this spread and see how well you do! If you have studied and memorized the key words, you should have no problem doing the reading.

A NEW LOVER

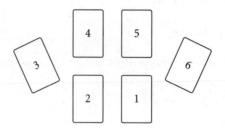

1. Will there be a new relationship for me soon?
2. What astrological sign will this person be?
3. Will we be compatible?
4. Will this be a lasting relationship?
5. Will this person be my soul mate?
6. What is the outcome of my desire?

A New Lover for Rachel

Cards in the Spread

1st position	Queen of Pentacles
2nd position	Ten of Pentacles
3rd position	King of Pentacles
4th position	Temperance
5th position	Seven of Wands (reversed)
6th position	Ace of Cups (reversed)

Reading

Question 1: Will there be a new relationship for me soon?

Answer: Queen of Pentacles. This Queen is involved with making money and is interested in health and healing. Rachel is an idealist and a perfectionist. She is now enrolled in college where she will meet lots of new people. Rachel is only seventeen, and quite shy. Thus, there is the potential for a relationship during the winter, but realistically, Rachel will be more focused on her studies.

Question 2: What astrological sign will this person be?

Answer: Ten of Pentacles. All pentacles refer to earth signs. Rachel is a Capricorn and perhaps she will attract an earth sign into her life.

Question 3: Will we be compatible?

Answer: King of Pentacles. This is an earth sign (Taurus). He would be compatible with Rachel as long as he is financially stable, practical, and sharing. Rachel seems interested in social services and she would like a partner who cares about others. Capricorns wish for success and can push their partners to attain their own goals.

Question 4: Will this be a lasting relationship?

Answer: Temperance. Rachel needs self-control, harmony, and balance. This card is ruled by Sagittarius, which is a freedom-loving sign. Sagittarians rarely stay in relationships for long periods of time, while learning about partners or mates takes time.

Question 5: Will this person be my soul mate?

Answer: Seven of Wands (reversed). This is the first reversed card in this spread. It represents feeling socially inferior or incompetent. The path is unclear for the future. Rachel may be disappointed with this individual and find he is not what she thought he was.

Question 6: What is the outcome of my desire?

Answer: Ace of Cups (reversed). Rachel does not foresee any new beginnings in love relationships for herself. There is emotional instability and she feels drained. She is ready to begin her first semester in college and feels uncertain. She would prefer waiting a year before entering college.

Comments

Rachel's parents insist she go to school or work. She does not drive, so working may be difficult. As a Capricorn, she is naturally inclined to focus on a career. A good education can teach her to become financially and emotionally independent. In conclusion, although a brief relationship is possible, it will take a back seat to the issues of work and school.

A New Lover for Denny

Cards in the Spread

1st position	Ace of Pentacles (reversed)
2nd position	Knight of Wands
3rd position	Five of Swords
4th position	Nine of Pentacles (reversed)
5th position	Page of Wands
6th position	Ten of Pentacles (reversed)

Reading

Question 1: Will there be a new relationship for me soon?

Answer: Ace of Pentacles (reversed). This card tells Denny that there will not be any new beginnings, especially in money matters. It takes money to go places and do things in a new relationship; now is a time to conserve resources and balance the budget.

Question 2: What astrological sign will this person be?

Answer: Knight of Wands. This Knight, a Leo, brings messages concerning work and social activities. Good news relating to work, a trip, or a change of residence. Relationships or other happy events are coming soon. If the new lover is a Leo, this person will expect attention—to be at center stage. Leos have great expectations, are very creative, and have a great sense of humor.

Question 3: Will we be compatible?

Answer: Five of Swords. Compatibility means getting along well with others. This card indicates that Denny creates his own problems and has the desire to overpower others due to his ego needs. This type of rash behavior may be the cause of his lack of friends and relationships. Denny has many desires and this clouds his judgment. Referring back to the previous card, Denny should be aware that Leos are extremely powerful people and they can be powerful adversaries.

Question 4: Will this be a lasting relationship?

Answer: Nine of Pentacles (reversed). Denny seems overly concerned with money matters. When reversed, this card indicates feelings of dependency. It also reflects a lack of wisdom gained through past experiences, loss through friends, or unwise investments. This relationship will last only if it does not affect Denny's finances.

Question 5: Will this person be my soul mate?

Answer: Page of Wands. This Page is a fire sign, as is the Leo from question two, eager to experience work and social life. He or she desires freedom and independence, and loves to travel. Denny stays close to home, is bound to his job, and will not spend his money without just cause. Perhaps they can share significant experiences and teach each other karmic lessons to polish each other's character.

Question 6: What is the outcome of my desire?

Answer: Ten of Pentacles (reversed). There will not be any significant change in Denny's financial picture, and his own issues preclude a happy new relationship. Denny's mental attitude must change; he must recognize that happiness is a choice.

Comments

Half of the cards in this spread are reversed, which shows a negative focus. Denny seems more interested in money and security than in a new and lasting relationship. He needs time to grow and mature and learn from life's experiences. Denny's values have not been formed and his sense of responsibility must be activated.

A ROMANTIC ATTRACTION

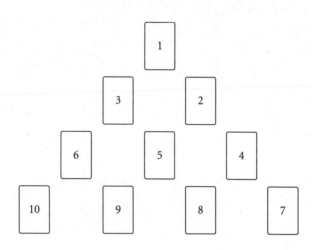

1. What is the attraction?
2. Is this person loving?
3. Can we have fun together?
4. Can we work together and support each other?
5. Will there be sexual compatibility?
6. Will our families get along?
7. Are there religious differences?
8. Will we have problems with power and money?
9. Is this a long-term relationship?
10. What is the outcome?

A Romantic Attraction for Susan

Cards in the Spread

1st position	The Sun
2nd position	Queen of Cups (reversed)
3rd position	Five of Wands
4th position	Two of Wands (reversed)
5th position	The High Priestess (reversed)
6th position	Two of Cups (reversed)
7th position	Nine of Pentacles (reversed)
8th position	Four of Swords
9th position	Nine of Swords
10th position	King of Cups (reversed)

Reading

Question 1: What is the attraction?

Answer: The Sun. Susan sees this man as open, honest, energetic, and youthful. He wants attention, has great expectations (not unreasonable, according to Susan), and wants to be a shining star.

Question 2: Is this person loving?

Answer: Queen of Cups (reversed). Susan feels he is intense but has an emotional drain regarding women. This Queen can be an implacable enemy—mean and hateful if wronged. This man does not love easily and may have been deeply hurt in the past.

Question 3: Can we have fun together?

Answer: Five of Wands. There could be ego problems between Susan and her new friend. This card indicates that Susan wants her way in work and socially. This could lead to confrontations between Susan and her new partner. Fighting can be fun, but is that the best way to build a relationship?

Question 4: Can we work together and support each other?

Answer: Two of Wands (reversed). Susan does not know how secure she is in this relationship. She does not know this person very well, nor has she known him for any length of time. They had an instant rapport, but unfortunately, he lives out of state, which poses problems. Susan said she did not know when she would see him again.

Question 5: Will there be sexual compatibility?

Answer: The High Priestess (reversed). Susan indicated that it was too early to be involved with this man in a sexually intimate way. She has some fears regarding this relationship and has decided to be cautious.

Question 6: Will our families get along?

Answer: Two of Cups (reversed). Susan feels that both families may try to come between her and her new love. This would create an emotional drain and force Susan and her partner to make decisions they are not ready to make. Susan must understand that a healthy, loving relationship is worth fighting for, regardless of family interference.

Question 7: Are there religious differences?

Answer: Nine of Pentacles (reversed). There are no problems with religious beliefs, but Susan feels she lacks wisdom with money and fears having to confront that issue. She does not feel like an independently wealthy woman and her new love comes from a very wealthy family.

Question 8: Will we have problems with power and money?

Answer: Four of Swords. Susan is creating her own problems and troubles. She must realize that her insecurities are driving her to distraction. Now is the time for her to rest, pray, and have faith in herself. If she and her new love are in balance, they can work out any problems.

Question 9: Is this a long-term relationship?

Answer: Nine of Swords. Susan is in crisis. She can only see problems and troubles in regards to this relationship. It is almost too good to be true—this man is young, attractive, and he has money. She may fear that she does not deserve this wonderful relationship, but why not? If Susan doesn't change her way of thinking, it will be over before she has a chance to get involved.

Question 10: What is the outcome?

Answer: King of Cups (reversed). Susan is feeling drained emotionally and is afraid of losing control. She has a fear of loving and giving her heart away and being hurt in the process. She may feel that she doesn't deserve love, but she must take a chance and believe that it will work.

Comments

Love, trust, and willingness are the answers to Susan's dilemma. Everyone deserves happiness in life and if money comes with it, all the better! However, since this reading, Susan has spent time with her love interest but the relationship has ended.

A Romantic Attraction for Larry

Cards in the Spread

1st position	Three of Swords
2nd position	King of Pentacles
3rd position	Ace of Wands (reversed)
4th position	Eight of Swords
5th position	Seven of Wands
6th position	Page of Pentacles
7th position	Six of Pentacles
8th position	The Lovers (reversed)
9th position	Page of Wands
10th position	Five of Pentacles

Reading

Question 1: What is the attraction?

Answer: Three of Swords. With this card, we see jealousy and problems, and a potential love triangle. Is this romantic attraction a married person? Does Larry seek out relationships with a person who is "unavailable," either emotionally or due to circumstances? Larry must like drama, but it can lead to serious confrontations and even injury.

Question 2: Is this person loving?

Answer: King of Pentacles. This individual is independent, loving, financially astute, and stubborn. She is not a dependent female but an experienced business person, good with money, and successful. She likes to help others in many different ways.

Question 3: Can we have fun together?

Answer: Ace of Wands (reversed). At this time, Larry is not happy because he does not have much free time to go on trips, begin new projects, or institute new experiences. This is not the time to make plans for a relationship. He needs to focus primarily on work and let his social life rest. However, if Larry can be light-hearted about this affair, then fun can be had with no harm to either party.

Question 4: Can we work together and support each other?

Answer: Eight of Swords. Larry has the strength to cope with this situation, but it may cause more problems than it is worth. He is on unsafe ground and does not want to recognize the danger. Larry should meditate and go within for answers to his questions. He must make his own decisions regarding this relationship.

Question 5: Will there be sexual compatibility?

Answer: Seven of Wands. Larry must use his own judgment and express his own ego and willpower. Question two spoke of the other person as being independent and stubborn. He can have compatibility if that is his desire, but it will likely require compromise.

Question 6: Will our families get along?

Answer: Page of Pentacles. If Larry is interested in schooling, or has a career focus or the potential to reach the top of his profession, he will be acceptable to the family of his romantic attraction. He must be ambitious, traditional, and a good provider with a positive attitude about making money.

Question 7: Are there religious differences?

Answer: Six of Pentacles. This card indicates that Larry must make some kind of choice regarding finances, being fair, and sharing resources. There could be religious differences between Larry and his love and they must both make adjustments.

Question 8: Will we have problems with power and money?

Answer: The Lovers (reversed). This card shows Larry has a lack of self-confidence, and may have problems with commitment. He is apprehensive about making decisions—perhaps he fears making wrong ones. Based on the other cards, it appears that problems with power and money could lead to alienation. Honesty and trust are essential ingredients in any relationship.

Question 9: Is this a long-term relationship?

Answer: Page of Wands. This Page is eager to experience work and a social life. Either Larry or the object of his romantic attraction desire freedom; both are headstrong and independent. They both wish to travel, study foreign cultures, and enjoy life. This relationship may be short and sweet or become a long-term affair that is "on again, off again."

Question 10: What is the outcome?

Answer: Five of Pentacles. This card indicates that either Larry or his romantic interest may get bogged down with too much work soon. Larry treats money as a god, which is not a healthy attitude and can cripple a person through negative beliefs. This card shows poverty-mindedness without any trust in an inner source. Perhaps neither Larry nor his love feel as supported as they wish to be. The potential for drug or alcohol abuse is indicated.

Comments

Any relationship can work if there is love, trust, and a desire to be together. There seem to be many difficulties to overcome in this relationship but, with perseverance, it can work out. If she is available, then Larry has a good chance to win the hand of the fair lady. If he cares, nothing will stand in his way!

LOVERS SPREAD

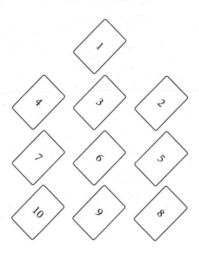

1. Does my lover care for me?
2. Are we compatible?
3. Do we have similar desires and goals?
4. Is my lover faithful and true?
5. Are we attracted to each other sexually only?
6. Will my lover consider marriage?
7. Does my lover have high standards and good values?
8. Can we share our finances and material possessions?
9. Will my lover stay with me or leave?
10. What is the final outcome?

Lovers Spread for Doris

Cards in the Spread

1st position	Temperance
2nd position	The Wheel of Fortune (reversed)
3rd position	Page of Cups
4th position	The Fool
5th position	Knight of Wands
6th position	The High Priestess (reversed)
7th position	The Hierophant (reversed)
8th position	Ten of Wands (reversed)
9th position	Ace of Cups
10th position	Four of Cups (reversed)

Reading

Question 1: Does my lover care for me?

Answer: Temperance. Doris, a Leo, must seek emotional balance during this difficult period of her life. Temperance shows fire, which is action and energy. She needs to slow down and enjoy her life, which is not easy for a fire sign. Doris' lover cares for her, but is not ready to commit to a lasting relationship. If she wants him, she must be patient—something that is against her nature.

Question 2: Are we compatible?

Answer: The Wheel of Fortune (reversed). There are no major changes ahead for Doris' relationship. She should not gamble or take any risks with her lover, but instead just go with the flow. Doris desires to be admired and loved, and her lover gives her what she needs when they are together.

Question 3: Do we have similar desires and goals?

Answer: Page of Cups. Both Doris and her lover are very sensitive, creative, and have psychic ability. This Page can bring good news regarding love relationships, parties, births, and marriages (not necessarily one's own). The card can also indicate that both Doris and her lover are immature, illusory, and possibly troubled with alcohol or drug problems. Their goals may not coincide.

Question 4: Is my lover faithful and true?

Answer: The Fool. Doris' lover wants adventure, new experiences, and being "out and about." Since there is no commitment, her lover is free to do as he pleases.

Question 5: Are we attracted to each other sexually only?

Answer: Knight of Wands. The Knight brings information concerning work and social activities. There are plans for a trip or change of residence. Doris is trying to do both—she is buying a condo and travels for her job. These activities do not give her much time to indulge in building a future for herself and her lover.

Question 6: Will my lover consider marriage?

Answer: The High Priestess (reversed). Doris does not think so. She feels he has a closed mind, fears commitment, and lacks self-confidence. He may not want an overly intelligent female in his life.

Question 7: Does my lover have high standards and good values?

Answer: The Hierophant (reversed). Doris thinks her lover is a pleasure seeker, indulgent, and materialistic. He enjoys sexual pleasures and being with Doris but does not seem to want a closer relationship. The Hierophant reversed shows a rebellious person who does not abide by the rules. If his standards and values are not high, Doris must re-evaluate this relationship.

Question 8: Can we share our finances and material possessions?

Answer: Ten of Wands (reversed). Doris feels burdened at this time with her own needs, including trying to buy a condo for herself. She may not be keen on sharing her resources without a show of good faith from her lover.

Question 9: Will my lover stay with me or leave?

Answer: Ace of Cups. This card tells Doris that she will have new beginnings in her love life. She will have a new residence within the year; happiness and pleasure will follow! This card also relates to new emotional involvements. Perhaps this lover will depart from Doris' life, making way for another, more compatible, relationship.

Question 10: What is the final outcome?

Answer: Four of Cups (reversed). Doris is disappointed in her love relationship; she has great expectations but fears commitment or rejection. She has been married and divorced and does not wish to repeat the experience.

Comments

With all the reversed cards in this spread, it does not seem likely that this relationship will continue and result in marriage. This agrees with Doris' thinking, but that can change in an instant—perhaps her real love is waiting in the wings? Since this reading, Doris has moved to Australia with a new love!

Lovers Spread for Suzanne

Cards in the Spread

1st position	Eight of Swords (reversed)
2nd position	The Tower (reversed)
3rd position	Nine of Cups
4th position	The Hierophant (reversed)
5th position	Knight of Wands
6th position	Seven of Pentacles (reversed)
7th position	Queen of Wands (reversed)
8th position	Judgement (reversed)
9th position	Six of Swords
10th position	Eight of Wands

Reading

Question 1: Does my lover care for me?

Answer: Eight of Swords (reversed). This card indicates that Suzanne should let go of this unhealthy relationship. Her lover does not have the stamina to maintain a good love relationship—or perhaps he or she is in ill health? There are problems in this relationship that must be addressed soon. This card may also show a lack of confidence or faith in herself.

Question 2: Are we compatible?

Answer: The Tower (reversed). She must evaluate her past experiences to see if she is repeating the same type of relationship; she may be refusing to give up old habit patterns. The focus is on sexuality, jealousy, and resentment, which could refer to her personally or to her lover. There may also be financial problems.

Question 3: Do we have similar desires and goals?

Answer: Nine of Cups. This is the wish card and it is upright—indicating that the wish Suzanne made at the beginning of the reading will be granted. She must use her intuition and wisdom gained through experience at this time. She feels both she and her lover want the same things and are working toward their goals.

Question 4: Is my lover faithful and true?

Answer: The Hierophant (reversed). This card in a reversed position indicates that her lover may be a pleasure-seeker, indulgent, and materialistic, as well as intolerant and judgmental. This person may have a closed mind and have little faith in him- or herself. In short, this lover may not be ready for a serious commitment.

Question 5: Are we attracted to each other sexually only?

Answer: Knight of Wands. This card infers that ego needs are the most important element in this relationship. There are messages coming to Suzanne; she has good news in store for her relating to a trip, a possible change of residence, or news of a marriage or celebration.

Question 6: Will my lover consider marriage?

Answer: Seven of Pentacles (reversed). This card shows an uncertain path to money and success is not assured. At this time, her lover is probably not willing to commit to a marriage. There may be more health problems; both Suzanne and her lover may feel frustration, anxiety, and a lack of confidence.

Question 7: Does my lover have high standards and good values?

Answer: Queen of Wands (reversed). This card corresponds with the ego and the need for attention, praise, and applause. Suzanne's lover may have high standards for himself and a sense of values that refer to him alone. This lover has great expectations that must be fulfilled by the other person. Suzanne may have a difficult time living up to his needs and expectations.

Question 8: Can we share our finances and material possessions?

Answer: Judgement (reversed). Either Suzanne or her lover is focused on material gain. There is a lack of judgment regarding each other and the inability to see truth in this relationship. They need to discuss their financial status honestly and learn to trust each other before there is any talk about commitment.

Question 9: Will my lover stay with me or leave?

Answer: Six of Swords. There is a temptation to run away from problems and Suzanne's lover is caught in a dilemma. The lover may not feel the relationship is worthwhile, nor does he desire a commitment now. Perhaps Suzanne or her lover should take a trip and try to see if "absence makes the heart grow fonder."

Question 10: What is the final outcome?

Answer: Eight of Wands. Suzanne has the strength to work toward her goals. She can overcome any problems if she desires.

Comments

This relationship has many problems, but they are not insurmountable. Communicate, and love will find a way!

MAGICAL LOVE

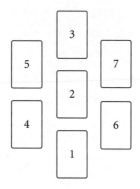

1. Will I ever find my true love?
2. Will I feel safe and secure with this person?
3. Is marriage a potential for me?
4. Will this new love be similar to my past lovers?
5. Will commitment be possible with this new love?
6. Can the magic last between us?
7. What can I do to make this person part of my life?

Magical Love for Denis

Cards in the Spread

1st position	The High Priestess (reversed)
2nd position	The Sun (reversed)
3rd position	Three of Pentacles
4th position	Nine of Cups (reversed)
5th position	Six of Cups (reversed)
6th position	Seven of Pentacles
7th position	Page of Pentacles (reversed)

Reading

Question 1: Will I ever find my true love?

Answer: The High Priestess (reversed). Denis says he does not know the meaning of life or how to build a good relationship. He has a closed mind and a fixed attitude. His parents were divorced when he was very young and now he fears a commitment. Denis could be too critical or overly analytical in his relationships with others.

Question 2: Will I feel safe and secure with this person?

Answer: The Sun (reversed). Denis will feel safe and secure with anyone only if he feels that way about himself. He lacks courage and may have low self-esteem. Denis must learn to accept himself first. He is a handsome young man and must have confidence in himself, be open and honest, and not fear rejection. Reversed, this card speaks of little ego and less energy—something that can be overcome.

Question 3: Is marriage a potential for me?

Answer: Three of Pentacles. The Three of Pentacles refers to the master craftsman—a very creative person who is successful in his or her chosen field. Denis makes money because he is good at his work. His talents will eventually bring him rich rewards, but he wants everything now. This card indicates that Denis wants a partner who has creative talents and can make money. Marriage is indeed a potential if he can find a female who supports herself and shares her resources with him.

Question 4: Will this new love be similar to my past lovers?

Answer: Nine of Cups (reversed). Denis is a Scorpio and very intense regarding his desires, but if he lacks the wisdom gained from past experiences in love, then he is doomed to repeat his past. If he is not aware of his emotional issues, he will bring the same type of relationship into his life. Without new information, or if he refuses to evaluate past experiences, repeat performances are inevitable in every area of his life. It is time to change deepseated beliefs.

Question 5: Will commitment be possible with this new love?

Answer: Six of Cups (reversed). This card reversed warns to be careful, as someone else is making decisions for you. If Denis is not making his own choices with this new love, he will feel trapped. There is a potential for this experience to be emotionally draining for Denis. Commitment is possible, but is it the best thing for him?

Question 6: Can the magic last between us?

Answer: Seven of Pentacles. The path to magic is financial for Denis. His mental focus is on financial responsibilities and feeling secure—having money in the bank. Life is magical, but people tend to look for flaws, making the magic disappear. If Denis loves himself and accepts himself, he can create a wonderful relationship in which the magic can last forever.

Question 7: What can I do to make this person part of my life?

Answer: Page of Pentacles (reversed). This Page is not interested in schooling, setting goals, or earning money. It indicates that Denis may want the easy life, preferring not to work too hard, and resenting authority figures. If Denis wants a lasting relationship, he must make some changes in his thinking. By paying attention to his thinking and beliefs, he can change his life. Remember: what you believe, you manifest. This is true for everyone.

Comments

Denis has had several relationships but none lasting. His parents were divorced and his early conditioning did not give him a feeling of security. Denis is thirty and does not feel successful. He has returned to medical school since this reading and hopes to become a physician's assistant. He has also entered into a new relationship, proving that he has begun to change his thinking.

Magical Love for Adele

Cards in the Spread

1st position	The Hanged Man
2nd position	Five of Pentacles (reversed)
3rd position	Ace of Wands
4th position	Ten of Pentacles
5th position	Ace of Pentacles (reversed)
6th position	The Hierophant
7th position	Queen of Swords (reversed)

Reading

Question 1: Will I ever find my true love?

Answer: The Hanged Man. Adele feels she has been sacrificed to the will and desires of others. She must learn to have faith in herself and stop living in fantasy. She will find true love only after she learns to love herself. She must also learn to meditate.

Question 2: Will I feel safe and secure with this person?

Answer: Five of Pentacles (reversed). Adele has not made money her god. She is surrounded by ambitious family members and wishes to live her life differently. At seventeen, she may feel she needs to get a job and be independent. If Adele enters into a relationship, she will accept this person on her terms, not based on what others want her to do. Adele is a Leo with a mind of her own and is beginning to have faith in her own talents. Feeling secure must come from within oneself.

Question 3: Is marriage a potential for me?

Answer: Ace of Wands. Marriage is always a potential for anyone who desires it. Adele is slated to have new beginnings in her work and social life. There will be new contacts for her and perhaps some new opportunities. She may crave excitement and attract someone new into her life, but love and marriage take time.

Question 4: Will this new love be similar to my past lovers?

Answer: Ten of Pentacles. Adele remarked that she was too young to have had a past lover. She is waiting to see the type of relationship she will attract. This card indicates a change of fortune and foretells better times ahead for her.

Question 5: Will commitment be possible with this new love?

Answer: Ace of Pentacles (reversed). The potential of this first relationship ending in commitment is not likely. The card signifies that Adele must conserve her resources during this period. Perhaps her first love will not have resources of his own and must finish school before making a commitment.

Question 6: Can the magic last between us?

Answer: The Hierophant. This card indicates Adele is looking for a teacher. At this time, Adele should seek her inner teacher and learn to meditate—going within herself to find answers to her problems. Her beliefs may be creating negative experiences in her life. She longs for approval and resents authority. The magic can last if she is not criticized in this relationship.

Question 7: What can I do to make this person part of my life?

Answer: Queen of Swords (reversed). Adele's mother, who has had a dramatic effect on her, is a Libra and so is this card. Adele has lived with her dad and stepmother the last few years and is not very happy with this arrangement. The Queen of Swords reversed shows that Adele does not wish to be alone; she prefers to be in a relationship. At this point, Adele must meet someone before she worries about how to make them a part of her life! She does not want to stay single for long, even though she is only seventeen.

Comments

Adele insisted on doing this particular reading. She is not involved with anyone but seems to be in a hurry to find someone who will love her and rescue her from her family. She had a rough childhood and has had problems as a teenager. She has two sisters and sibling rivalry may be part of the issue. Time will tell whether she changes her thinking and beliefs and decides to have a good life in spite of her past experiences. Currently, Adele has an apartment with a female roommate. She works and goes to college. She's a nonconformist in her appearance, with a shaved head and rings in her ears, nose, and tongue.

Magical Love for Julie

Cards in the Spread

1st position	Page of Wands
2nd position	The World (reversed)
3rd position	The High Priestess
4th position	Five of Pentacles
5th position	Seven of Pentacles
6th position	King of Swords
7th position	Queen of Pentacles

Reading

Question 1: Will I ever find my true love?

Answer: Page of Wands. Julie is a Sagittarius and this card represents her. She loves freedom and new experiences, is independent, and desires to travel. Perhaps Julie does not want a permanent relationship due to her need for freedom. She disclosed her desire to find a younger man.

Question 2: Will I feel safe and secure with this person?

Answer: The World (reversed). No. The financial picture does not look promising. Julie will not feel supported and this will create problems.

Question 3: Is marriage a potential for me?

Answer: The High Priestess. The High Priestess says Julie is intelligent and has the answers within herself. She will know intuitively whether a relationship is right.

Question 4: Will this new love be similar to my past lovers?

Answer: Five of Pentacles. The Five of Pentacles suggests that the lover desires money and may be into alcohol or drugs, or crippled in some way—physically or emotionally. The belief in money rather than putting faith in oneself is not positive. Julie must ask herself if her past relationships had money problems.

Question 5: Will commitment be possible with this new lover?

Answer: Seven of Pentacles. The Seven of Pentacles reveals Julie's desire to be in charge of her own money and its dispersal. She works for her money and does not want anyone to tell her what to do with it. This card does not indicate commitment unless it is on Julie's terms.

Question 6: Can the magic last between us?

Answer: King of Swords. This card may refer to legal proceedings or her lover (a Gemini). Julie desires a partner with career potential and intelligence. In this case, the magic seems to be in the finances rather than in love. A prenuptial agreement can further dampen the magic.

Question 7: What can I do to make this person part of my life?

Answer: Queen of Pentacles. With the Queen of Pentacles, sex and money seem to be the solution. Julie feels if she had more money, she would attract a lover, but she doesn't want to share her resources or be dependent. This is a dilemma!

Comments

Julie needs to examine her emotional needs. Her need for independence and fear of vulnerability are hampering her ability to attract a healthy relationship. She needs to trust her partner and herself.

GUIDE FOR LOVERS

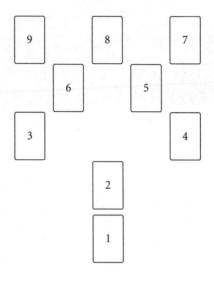

1. What type of mate am I seeking?
2. Will this person be nurturing, loving, and supportive?
3. Will communication be a problem between us?
4. Does this person work or have a career?
5. Will our attraction be sexual, emotional, or mental?
6. Are we mature enough to have a serious relationship?
7. Will our religious beliefs be compatible?
8. What financial difficulties might there be?
9. What can I do to bring this person into my life?

Three
Home and Family Issues

The spreads in this chapter are:

Family Problems

Health

A Thief in the Home

Lost Articles

Family issues are important to each person and the Family Problems spread can show how matters began and how they have escalated. The Health spread can inform individuals how they are punishing themselves due to long-held beliefs.

A Thief in the Home came about during a conversation with a friend who was very upset after being robbed and needed to release his anger. It was then the spread was born. Inspiration comes from many directions and we must be open to this potential.

The final example in this chapter is the Lost Articles spread. It does not have a sample reading, but is fairly clear. The questions may jog the querents' memory, reminding them where they placed the item.

Remember, each spread is serious to the querent. As a reader, you must try to lighten the querent's burdens by providing pertinent information the person can use.

FAMILY PROBLEMS

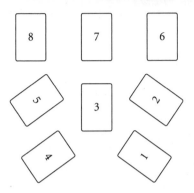

1. Who is primarily involved with the problem?
2. What is the conflict regarding your security or safety?
3. How is dysfunctional behavior an issue in the problem?
4. Has this person had similar problems in the past?
5. What steps must be taken to resolve this matter?
6. Are there situations you should avoid?
7. What effect do these problems have on your health?
8. What are the end results?

Family Problems for Tom

Cards in the Spread

1st position   Ten of Wands (reversed)
2nd position   Nine of Pentacles (reversed)
3rd position   The World
4th position   Seven of Swords
5th position   Nine of Wands
6th position   Eight of Swords
7th position   Eight of Cups (reversed)
8th position   Six of Wands (reversed)

Reading

Question 1: Who is primarily involved with the problem?

Answer: Ten of Wands (reversed). Tom feels he carries heavy burdens at work and socially. He spoke of his frustrations with obstacles presented by others. All the people involved are family, and Tom thinks he is trapped in the situation. He does not see the possibility of changes at the present time.

Question 2: What is the conflict regarding your security or safety?

Answer: Nine of Pentacles (reversed). Tom is realizing his lack of wisdom in money matters. He does not think the family backs him in his decisions, but feels dependent because his money is tied up in the family business.

Question 3: How is dysfunctional behavior an issue in the problem?

Answer: The World. One member of the family has back problems, which is creating emotional turmoil, and another is not carrying a fair share of the responsibilities, according to Tom. But with the World card here, it is indicated that success in all endeavors will be the outcome. Tom has support from his inner resources and can maintain balance through any crisis.

Question 4: Has this person had similar problems in the past?

Answer: Seven of Swords. Tom remarked that problems are part of the ongoing picture. The individual with back problems has had them before, and the other person was not interested in tying himself down to work. Tom feels cheated or that others are stealing from him. However, the situation may be temporary and can change quickly.

Question 5: What steps must be taken to resolve this matter?

Answer: Nine of Wands. Tom needs to apply wisdom at work and in his relationships with others. He must use fair tactics and achieve his goals through intelligence, while learning to protect himself and his interests.

Question 6: Are there situations you should avoid?

Answer: Eight of Swords. There is no way for Tom to avoid his problems. He feels in bondage and on unsafe ground, but he will get his footing soon. Fortunately, he has the strength to cope with his situation and should look within for answers. Tom must take care to maintain his health in order to keep the business flourishing.

Question 7: What effect do these problems have on your health?

Answer: Eight of Cups (reversed). Tom cannot leave this situation. At this time, he feels all right but the emotional drain will have an effect eventually.

Question 8: What are the end results?

Answer: Six of Wands (reversed). Tom must take care not to make unwise choices due to his frustrations. Avoiding setbacks by taking right actions is important, and negative use of energy will create worse problems. Tom should be prepared for delays and frustrations until he can set new plans in motion.

Comments

It is difficult to separate a family involved with business—everyone must share the blame when problems arise. In this case, the family issues are tied to a business in which these people are involved. Matters have become so intense that the health of at least one member and the emotional body of another have been affected. The only solution is to "wait and see;" otherwise, the financial aspect of the business will suffer and everyone will lose.

Family Problems for Gerry

Cards in the Spread

1st position	Seven of Cups (reversed)
2nd position	The Fool (reversed)
3rd position	Nine of Cups
4th position	King of Pentacles (reversed)
5th position	Ace of Cups (reversed)
6th position	Knight of Swords (reversed)
7th position	Page of Pentacles
8th position	Two of Wands (reversed)

Reading

Question 1: Who is primarily involved with the problem?

Answer: Seven of Cups (reversed). Gerry feels negative because her emotional needs are not being fulfilled. She is not using her abilities for creative visualization, which might help her get over this negativity. There is a potential for abuse of drugs or alcohol, which could be part of the problem within the family.

Question 2: What is the conflict regarding your security or safety?

Answer: The Fool (reversed). Gerry does not want to do anything foolish, but she is anxious about her financial status and her health. Staying stuck in a negative situation is not positive.

Question 3: How is dysfunctional behavior an issue in the problem?

Answer: Nine of Cups. This is the wish card and when it comes up, it means the person will get his or her wish. Gerry was pleased to hear this. She is gaining wisdom through her experiences, which will help her in future relationships. She is also gaining confidence in her emotional life. If drugs or alcohol are involved, she will know how to handle the situation without feeling like a victim. As they say, "Experience is the best teacher."

Question 4: Has this person had similar problems in the past?

Answer: King of Pentacles (reversed). This indicates someone who is lazy, selfish, a speculator, and impractical with money. This person may be dishonest and can use shady business practices. Gerry sees this individual in her family as someone who is sensual, loving luxury and desiring pleasure. He is not willing to share resources, and Gerry feels unloved. He will not change and Gerry must make her own decisions about what is best for her.

Question 5: What steps must be taken to resolve this matter?

Answer: Ace of Cups (reversed). Gerry does not see any new beginnings in her life at this time. She is feeling an emotional drain and her love is turning into bitterness. Gerry will soon need to make some decisions, discuss the matter openly with this individual, or leave. Confrontation is sometimes the only way to resolve a situation.

Question 6: Are there situations you should avoid?

Answer: Knight of Swords (reversed). This Knight carries news of problems and troubles, but his message may be an unreliable source of information. Gerry must avoid becoming depressed or feeling like a victim. She can always make a decision to leave the situation and go out on her own, away from the family. The ties that bind can be severed!

Question 7: What effect do these problems have on your health?

Answer: Page of Pentacles. This Page refers to the student. By going to school and getting a better education, Gerry's life can improve. Now is the time for a change in focus to something positive, which will also keep her healthy.

Question 8: What are the end results?

Answer: Two of Wands (reversed). Gerry does not have enough confidence in herself. She needs more education—she feels she doesn't know her work or her place in society. She is afraid of failure and perhaps needs to return to her family, but she does not want that to happen. This indicates that Gerry must cultivate her ambition and strength of will to strike out on her own.

Comments

Looking at the cards in this spread and seeing that six cards are reversed lets the reader understand that the person has a negative outlook on life. There is fear and guilt within this mind, which causes Gerry to be overly cautious in her actions. Lack of self-confidence and an inferiority complex are playing large parts in her life, as well. Before Gerry can learn to enjoy life and be happy, she must first change her thinking.

HEALTH SPREAD

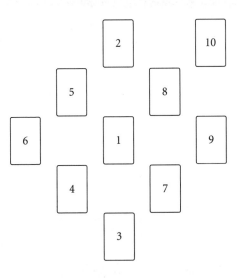

1. Should I worry about my health?
2. How do I overcome my fears?
3. Will I ever be happy?
4. Past feelings of guilt and resentment?
5. Past feelings of depression or unhappiness?
6. Past health problems?
7. Do I need formal medical attention?
8. Will my physical health affect my financial health?
9. Will spiritual awareness aid in overcoming any health problem?
10. Outcome?

Health Spread for Cory

Cards in the Spread

1st position	Knight of Wands
2nd position	Three of Pentacles
3rd position	Judgement
4th position	Nine of Wands (reversed)
5th position	The Devil (reversed)
6th position	The High Priestess
7th position	Eight of Cups (reversed)
8th position	Ace of Cups (reversed)
9th position	Queen of Wands (reversed)
10th position	The Star

Reading

Question 1: Should I worry about my health?

Answer: Knight of Wands. Cory is receiving positive messages regarding work and social activities. His health is fine; there is nothing to worry about.

Question 2: How do I overcome my fears?

Answer: Three of Pentacles. This is the card of the master craftsman who makes money because he is good at what he does. The number three refers to creative visualization, which can be used to overcome any problem or fear. Cory must think about his worth when it comes to earning money.

Question 3: Will I ever be happy?

Answer: Judgement. It will be up to Cory to make himself happy. Awareness and understanding must be used, and being in touch with the inner self is important. As Cory put it, "Arise from the grave of ignorance."

Question 4: Past feelings of guilt and resentment?

Answer: Nine of Wands (reversed). Cory says he did not use wisdom gained through his experience at work and is now suing his boss for wrongful termination. The allegations have created some health problems for Cory, but nothing long-lasting. He did not protect himself at work with his employers, and there was a great deal of jealousy with the other staff. Cory had many steady customers who appreciated his dedication to service.

Question 5: Past feelings of depression or unhappiness?

Answer: The Devil (reversed). Cory is not willing to chain himself to the Devil for materialistic gain. He has been in spiritual work most of his life and when negative experiences happen, he is shocked. He has become unhappy due to his character being maligned, and some of his friends have caused him to feel depressed. Crisis periods can relieve boredom and Cory needed a change whether he was aware of it or not.

Question 6: Past health problems?

Answer: The High Priestess. The High Priestess knows all about health and everything else. Cory has good health with no history of major illness. Because he believes in health as a natural outcome of life, he does not bring negative thoughts about health into his life.

Question 7: Do I need formal medical attention?

Answer: Eight of Cups (reversed). When Cory doesn't have the strength to turn his back on an emotional situation, he takes an aspirin. He told me during the reading that he drinks alcohol occasionally to combat an overabundance of sensitive feelings. He is very open psychically and tends to "pick up" on other people's thoughts. He claims that meditation helps him overcome negativity around him.

Question 8: Will my physical health affect my financial health?

Answer: Ace of Cups (reversed). This card shows an emotional drain and no new beginnings. Cory does not like inactivity! He will initiate new experiences, including financial ones, through his will. Being spiritually aware, Cory knows only "wellness" and is focused on this attitude.

Question 9: Will spiritual awareness aid in overcoming any health problem?

Answer: Queen of Wands (reversed). Cory has a need for ego-recognition and wants attention. He is an Aquarian and this is a Leo card (these signs are the opposites of each other). However, his spiritual understanding keeps him from going overboard in his desires and his attitude keeps his health problems to a minimum.

Question 10: Outcome?

Answer: The Star. Cory must set new goals and "hitch his wagon to a star." He should raise his expectations to create a healthy environment. There is a potential for new directions in Cory's life.

Comments

If Cory continues his spiritual inclinations, he will stay healthy. The trial is over and he won! He is going to school for training in a new career.

Health Spread for Lacie

Cards in the Spread

1st position	Ten of Cups
2nd position	Ace of Swords (reversed)
3rd position	Three of Cups (reversed)
4th position	Temperance (reversed)
5th position	Death (reversed)
6th position	Four of Pentacles (reversed)
7th position	The Lovers
8th position	Five of Swords
9th position	Four of Swords (reversed)
10th position	Seven of Swords (reversed)

Reading

Question 1: Should I worry about my health?

Answer: Ten of Cups. Lacie will have major changes in her life affecting her love and emotions. She needs back surgery, not for the first time. (Sword and pentacle cards can indicate health problems and potential operations.) Worry does not solve anything; having faith does.

Question 2: How do I overcome my fears?

Answer: Ace of Swords (reversed). This card indicates no new beginnings in problems because the old ones are not finished. Lacie has had two back surgeries on the same disc and now needs a third, which is dangerous. Any back problems indicate a lack of support. Lacie is a Capricorn and a very determined person. The way to overcome fear is to have faith in one's inner source.

Question 3: Will I ever be happy?

Answer: Three of Cups (reversed). This card shows that Lacie does not make herself happy. She is having problems in her relationships, which is creating an emotional drain with the potential for depression and loneliness. Lacie and her husband spend too much time in their business and do not have much time for a social life.

Question 4: Past feelings of guilt and resentment?

Answer: Temperance (reversed). Lacie is self-indulgent, restless, and lacking patience. Her desires can lead to waste, loss, or misfortune at this time. Her negative attitude has resulted from past feelings of guilt and resentment.

Question 5: Past feelings of depression or unhappiness?

Answer: Death (reversed). Lacie is in her sixties and has four children of her own and three children from her second marriage. She has been through some difficult and depressing times. By holding onto these negative experiences, a person has the tendency to repeat them. If Lacie has a materialistic focus, which is natural to Capricorns, she must decide when she feels secure enough to relax and be happy. Lacie's back problems are rooted in her past and have again recently manifested.

Question 6: Past health problems?

Answer: Four of Pentacles (reversed). Lacie has had other medical problems and visits the doctor quite frequently. This card indicates a potential to have health problems due to financial matters, but money problems have not always been the cause of her health afflictions. Lacie has a tendency to have fixed ideas; she is very traditional and does not realize that she is responsible for her condition.

Question 7: Do I need formal medical attention?

Answer: The Lovers. This card refers to choices that must be made regarding health matters. Lacie has decided to have a third operation on her back to relieve the pain. She refuses to listen to any alternative suggestions and must take responsibility for her actions.

Question 8: Will my physical health affect my financial health?

Answer: Five of Swords. At this time, Lacie does not have a healthy attitude. She meets the public every day and must wear a happy face. However, Lacie is in constant pain and this makes it difficult to maintain a pleasant demeanor with customers. Her financial affairs will be negatively affected if her operation keeps her bedridden for any length of time. Her husband will need other people to help run their business, which will cut into their profits.

Question 9: Will spiritual awareness aid in overcoming any health problems?

Answer: Four of Swords (reversed). This card indicates that Lacie does not realize her problems and troubles. She is burning the candle at both ends. Lacie and her husband say they cannot find good help. Neither of them is interested in spiritual responsibility or information that could change their lives.

Question 10: Outcome?

Answer: Seven of Swords (reversed). This card reveals that there will be no victory regarding Lacie's problems. The situation is stagnant, and there is potential for jealousy and a lack of love and harmony. Lacie feels she is in an unhappy relationship that may never end. The path she is taking is material, which shows a lack of faith in her inner source. Lacie should re-evaluate her situation and seek answers she may have overlooked. Peace and happiness are always attainable.

Comments

This situation concerning Lacie, her husband, and their business must be resolved in order for her health to improve. Lacie and her husband must spend less time working and more time playing. When they straighten out their finances and the time they spend at work, life could be beautiful!

A THIEF IN THE HOME

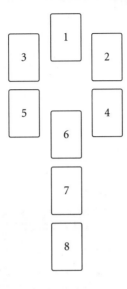

1. Why did I/we attract a thief into the home?
2. Is this thief related to me or my spouse?
3. Is it possible the thief will return?
4. Would an alarm system help in the future?
5. What can I/we do now to change the feelings in the home?
6. What responsibilities did I/we overlook?
7. What did I/we learn from this experience?
8. The outcome?

A Thief in the Home for Stephen

Cards in the Spread

1st position	Two of Wands
2nd position	Six of Cups
3rd position	The Chariot
4th position	Knight of Pentacles
5th position	Queen of Swords
6th position	The Sun
7th position	Three of Cups
8th position	Eight of Wands (reversed)

Reading

Question 1: Why did we attract a thief into the home?

Answer: Two of Wands. Stephen knows his work and social life. He has the world in his hands and has worked hard to attain this position, but he may fear that he does not deserve all the good coming his way.

Question 2: Is this thief related to me or my spouse?

Answer: Six of Cups. Stephen thinks the thief is someone he knows and may be distantly related to his wife. This card can indicate someone returning from the past, which could be a relative. He gave this person a key to their home, which was an irresponsible action. Stephen and his wife need to be more discriminating and responsible in the future.

Question 3: Is it possible the thief will return?

Answer: The Chariot. This card indicates victory. By controlling his desires and guiding himself mentally, Stephen will be successful. He must meditate and turn to his higher self to find out why he attracted the thief in the first place. This can bring positive results to overcome negative experiences.

Question 4: Would an alarm system help in the future?

Answer: Knight of Pentacles. This Knight brings positive messages concerning money. If Stephen and his wife want to install an alarm system, they will be able to afford it. However, if they continue to give keys away, the alarm system will be useless.

Question 5: What can you do now to change the feelings in the home?

Answer: Queen of Swords. This card refers to problems and often indicates a divorced or widowed woman. Stephen is married to a divorced woman and she is now pregnant with their first child. They both feel violated by this thief and are trying to decide what to do. Perhaps the marriage is not as smooth as it should be and both partners are feeling pressured. It is time to evaluate their feelings and be honest with each other.

Question 6: What responsibilities did we overlook?

Answer: The Sun. Stephen needs confidence in his abilities to make life work out. He must be open to new thoughts and have the courage to carry through. Stephen must seek truth, use his creative talents, and bring success into his life now.

Question 7: What did you learn from this experience?

Answer: Three of Cups. This card refers to pregnancy, a celebration, and good use of creative talents. Stephen has the desire to be happy and enjoy his marriage while he awaits the arrival of his first child. His emotions are positive and he loves his wife. The lesson is learning to think positively and be responsible.

Question 8: The outcome?

Answer: Eight of Wands (reversed). Stephen lacks strength socially or in his work and feels that the delays and setbacks in his life are keeping him from success. Stephen feels insecure and his thinking is not balanced. He is focused on one particular person being responsible and is not interested in hearing about the possibility of anyone else being the thief.

Comments

Unfortunately, Stephen has been robbed again since this reading. He is a healer and has worked very hard to be successful in his career. He is in his forties and married for the first time—something he did not expect to happen. As a bonus, they recently had a son. Stephen's life has changed dramatically in less than a year and he now has new responsibilities that may be overwhelming for him. Stephen will make it through with flying colors if he gives himself the opportunity.

LOST ARTICLES SPREAD

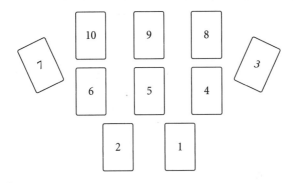

1. What is lost?
2. When did you discover it missing?
3. When was the last time you saw the article?
4. Is it possible you misplaced the article?
5. Should you contact the police?
6. Do you feel guilty or responsible for losing the article?
7. Was the article of sentimental value?
8. Was the article of financial value?
9. Do you have insurance for lost property?
10. Will the article be found soon?

Four

Finances

In this chapter, all the spreads concern a person's finances in one way or another.

The spreads are:

Business

Career

Lawsuit

Money

Work

Legal Matters 2

At this writing, all the people involved with these spreads are still trying to resolve their problems. The Lawsuit case is still pending, the Business spread querents are doing their best, and the individuals in the Money spread are still struggling. Only time will tell if these people manage to overcome their dilemmas.

The Legal Matters 2 spread does not have a sample reading and you can test your skills with it. There was not another individual available who was involved with a legal battle when the spread was developed.

BUSINESS SPREAD

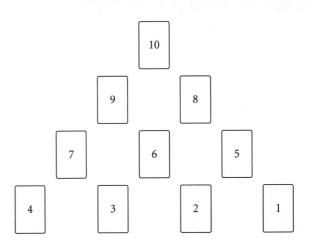

1. Should I begin my own business?
2. Should the business be a partnership?
3. Will the public be receptive to my product?
4. Will the work be difficult?
5. Are there changes I need to make now?
6. Are there responsibilities I have overlooked?
7. Will I be successful?
8. Will I make money through this business?
9. What method of advertising should I use?
10. Final outcome?

Business Spread for Sam

Cards in the Spread

1st position	Queen of Pentacles
2nd position	Queen of Wands
3rd position	Page of Swords (reversed)
4th position	Nine of Cups
5th position	The Hermit
6th position	Seven of Pentacles (reversed)
7th position	King of Wands (reversed)
8th position	Two of Cups
9th position	Page of Pentacles
10th position	The Fool (reversed)

Reading

Question 1: Should I begin my own business?

Answer: Queen of Pentacles. This card symbolizes making money and being critical or judgmental. Sam has started his own business, which has been time-consuming and demanding. It has already created a health problem for him that he, fortunately, has overcome.

Question 2: Should the business be a partnership?

Answer: Queen of Wands. Sam has two partners and is not comfortable in this position. One partner might have been fine, but not two. Sam is ambitious and he is seeking success at work and in his social life. His ego needs are involved with this business and he wants admiration and attention.

Question 3: Will the public be receptive to my product?

Answer: Page of Swords (reversed). This card indicates that Sam does not pay attention to his problems. The public has been receptive to the products and the business is doing well. Even so, Sam is anxious and seems to neglect his personal life.

Question 4: Will the work be difficult?

Answer: Nine of Cups. This is the "wish card" and, when upright in a spread, says, "Your wish will be granted." Sam has plenty of confidence in his work and is able to put in long hours periodically. The work itself is not difficult.

Question 5: Are there changes I need to make now?

Answer: The Hermit. Sam owned a business for thirty years, but not in the same field. He has gathered wisdom through that experience and can apply some of that knowledge to his new venture. The partners are enlarging the store to accommodate more customers, so the changes are being made now.

Question 6: Are there responsibilities I have overlooked?

Answer: Seven of Pentacles (reversed). This card symbolizes an uncertain path to money. The number seven can pertain to legal matters, as well. Sam is an Aries, and they usually have good ideas, but they don't always stay for the finish. Sam must accept responsibility, and he must learn to share with the other partners. There may be pettiness and jealousy among the partners now.

Question 7: Will I be successful?

Answer: King of Wands (reversed). This King is an Aries, as is Sam. If he is being childish, selfish, domineering, and a petty tyrant, then the other partners will work against him. Causing relationship problems or being overbearing and unyielding will not bring success; working together for the common good will.

Question 8: Will I make money through this business?

Answer: Two of Cups. Sam understands that a good relationship is healthy, characterized by honesty and give-and-take. If he can keep his ego in check, the business, which has shown its potential in the last few years, could prosper.

Question 9: What method of advertising should I use?

Answer: Page of Pentacles. This Page is a Capricorn—the student who goes to school to learn about a career. Capricorn (earth) and Aries (fire) can work well together. The fire takes action and earth provides follow-through. Capricorn is financially focused and Aries, as a rule, has great ideas about making money. Targeting advertising toward schools or young people in general could be very effective. Hiring young people to work with the customers is another possibility. Sam should experiment with different methods to learn which work best.

Question 10: Final outcome?

Answer: The Fool (reversed). This card symbolizes balance. Sam must balance his emotional needs, especially his ego. He must curb his anxieties, have faith in the future, act maturely, and be responsible if he wants his business to succeed. Sam fears being made a fool of, which keeps him unsettled.

Comments

Sam's business is doing very well. The problems seem to stem from Sam's interactions with his partners. If they do not resolve these issues, their chances of success will be greatly reduced. Life is about people living and working together in harmony. Let's hope these three learn this lesson soon.

Business Spread for Donald

Cards in the Spread

1st position	Five of Cups
2nd position	Ten of Wands
3rd position	Five of Wands
4th position	The Tower
5th position	The World
6th position	The Star
7th position	Judgement
8th position	The Wheel of Fortune
9th position	Seven of Wands
10th position	Nine of Wands (reversed)

Reading

Question 1: Should I begin my own business?

Answer: Five of Cups. Don believes in love but his love is not based in truth. There is the potential for his relationship to suffer due to job-related stress. Don started his own business several years ago and he spends long hours at his work. He is not sure about keeping the business if it threatens his marriage.

Question 2: Should the business be a partnership?

Answer: Ten of Wands. This card indicates that there will be major changes in Don's life, which could include new business methods or new opportunities. Perhaps if Don had a partner, he could share the burdens at work.

Question 3: Will the public be receptive to my product?

Answer: Five of Wands. Don has good products and is proud of his business, but his ego may cause problems. He wants his own way and, if he decides to take a partner, there could be conflicts of will and power struggles.

Question 4: Will the work be difficult?

Answer: The Tower. Don must overthrow his false ideas and get rid of his childish habit patterns. The work is not difficult at this time but, with the additions Don wants to make, it could become so. This would create more strife and discord in his relationship.

Question 5: Are there changes I need to make now?

Answer: The World. Don would be wise to understand that success is possible in all of his endeavors. If he knew that he was being supported by his inner source, he could relax and allow himself to enjoy the fruits of his labor now. He needs to have more faith in himself, become more balanced, and trust his ability to succeed.

Question 6: Are there responsibilities I have overlooked?

Answer: The Star. The Star symbolizes goals for the future. Perhaps Don needs to set new goals, accept new opportunities, and be optimistic about the future. There are also relationship obligations that must be taken into account. Success at the cost of relationships is not a positive trade-off.

Question 7: Will I be successful?

Answer: Judgement. Don has the potential to be very successful. With new understanding comes more self-confidence. Accepting one's inner source and realizing that there is always help will bring joy and happiness into one's life. Don's health could improve as he becomes aware of his potential. He may move his residence, take a trip, or just learn to relax.

Question 8: Will I make money through this business?

Answer: The Wheel of Fortune. Now is the time for Don to take a chance, make changes, seek new experiences, and enjoy his family and other relationships. If Don can maintain a positive outlook, he will stay healthy and happy—and make money.

Question 9: What method of advertising should I use?

Answer: Seven of Wands. This card indicates that Don should rely on his own judgment. He wants to express his ego at work and would prefer magazine ads, as well as direct personal contact with potential customers.

Question 10: Final outcome?

Answer: Nine of Wands (reversed). Don must have more confidence in the business and himself. There could be interference from outside sources, or even from family. Don may be encountering jealousy and negative feelings from his wife or others around him.

Comments

Success is there, but Don must feel he deserves it. He must balance his responsibility to the business with his responsibility to maintain a healthy relationship at home.

CAREER SPREAD

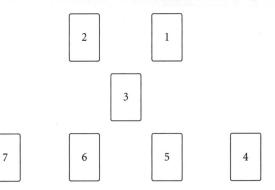

1. Is the career I have chosen what I really want?
2. What steps can I take to improve my career?
3. Are there aspects to my career I cannot change?
4. Am I doing my best in my career?
5. What changes can I make personally that will help my career?
6. What blocks in my past are affecting my career now?
7. Outcome?

Career Spread for Janice

Cards in the Spread

1st position	The Chariot
2nd position	Five of Swords
3rd position	The Moon
4th position	Knight of Cups
5th position	Nine of Cups (reversed)
6th position	The High Priestess (reversed)
7th position	The Emperor

Reading

Question 1: Is the career I have chosen what I really want?

Answer: The Chariot. The career path Janice took was her own carefully considered choice. She enjoys her work.

Question 2: What steps can I take to improve my career?

Answer: Five of Swords. Janice is aware of her problems and troubles but continually brings more of the same into her life, especially at work. She needs to control her speech and temper for better results. Others may find her aggressive manner difficult to deal with. Janice must learn to balance her ego needs with patience and understanding.

Question 3: Are there aspects to my career I cannot change?

Answer: The Moon. Janice may have unrealistic expectations, and her emotions are in overdrive. When an individual works for the government, as Janice does, he or she is not able to make career changes on a whim. Movement is only possible if positions become open. In addition, there may be forces at work behind the scenes, of which Janice is not aware.

Question 4: Am I doing my best in my career?
Answer: Knight of Cups. Messages are coming to Janice that indicate she is doing a good job. She has fifty people working for her in her department and most of them feel she is a good boss. Her fears are due to her own insecurities.

Question 5: What changes can I make personally that will help my career?
Answer: Nine of Cups (reversed). Janice has many wishes concerning her job, but they will not materialize at this time. There is also a lack of wisdom in love, which affects her emotional state. Janice needs more faith in her dealings with other people. It would be wise of her to love and accept others and herself.

Question 6: What blocks in my past are affecting my career now?
Answer: The High Priestess (reversed). This card reversed reveals a closed mind and a fear of new information. Janice can be stubborn, superficial, and opinionated. She did not feel supported by her parents when she was a child and set out to prove to them that she could be successful—and she is. Her parents are both deceased, but old habit patterns are hard to break. This card, when it appears in a spread for a female, may indicate a need to

accept the dependent side of her own nature to create a balance within.

Question 7: Outcome?

Answer: The Emperor. The Emperor is dressed for war, but he is sitting passively. He realizes that he can always fight, but he is going to think before he makes any decisions. This is good advice for Janice, a mature woman with grown children. Maturity comes through experience and then applying the knowledge one has gained. The business world is usually controlled by the male population and this is true in Janice's field. For Janice, change will occur only if the boss gets transferred or dies. She must remember to enjoy her life and be proud of her position because she has come a long way.

Comments

Janice has done a great deal with her life. She raised her two children without help from her ex-husband, and she finished her education while she worked. Now she has a good job as a CPA. She must learn to respect and value her accomplishments.

Career Spread for Harvey

Cards in the Spread

1st position	Four of Wands
2nd position	Judgement
3rd position	Page of Swords
4th position	The High Priestess (reversed)
5th position	The Magician (reversed)
6th position	The Hanged Man
7th position	Three of Wands

Reading

Question 1: Is the career I have chosen what I really want?

Answer: Four of Wands. This card indicates a fruitful life, happiness, and balance between work and social life. Being an Aries, Harvey does not enjoy being tied down in any one place for long. He feels his choices are not always fruitful or balanced. He has had many job changes in the last year and has not focused on future goals.

Question 2: What steps can I take to improve my career?

Answer: Judgement. Awareness and awakening to truth are both represented by the Judgement card. Harvey should learn all he can about his work, then he will reap his rewards. Harvey is impatient, another Aries trait, and wants to experience everything now. He must pay attention to his inner self—understanding does not occur overnight.

Question 3: Are there aspects to my career I cannot change?

Answer: Page of Swords. This card indicates that Harvey will not pay attention to his own problems but will try to solve other people's difficulties. He can be a friend to the world, but at what cost? This card suggests that Harvey is not as mature as he thinks. In order to make any changes in his life, he must first change himself.

Question 4: Am I doing my best in my career?

Answer: The High Priestess (reversed). The High Priestess reversed can indicate fear, guilt, and a refusal to go inside oneself to find truth. Harvey may not be open to new information, tending instead to be closed-minded or prejudiced. He remarked that he felt he was going nowhere with his present attitude. Harvey is not doing his best work due to a lack of self-confidence and self-awareness.

Question 5: What changes can I make personally that will help my career?

Answer: The Magician (reversed). Harvey desires a new job but must wait until something becomes available in his field. He is frustrated and would like to force the issue and cause changes, but this is not positive at this time. One major change he can make is to control his impulsiveness.

Question 6: What blocks in my past are affecting my career now?

Answer: The Hanged Man. The Hanged Man suggests that Harvey needs to completely reverse his attitude. He needs to shed his illusions, along with old, negative habit patterns. He may have a tendency to retreat into alcohol or drugs, or to indulge in feeling like a victim or martyr. Meditation—quieting the mind in order to see truth— would help him get in touch with and release his blocks.

Question 7: Outcome?

Answer: Three of Wands. This card says, "I make or create my work and social activities." It indicates that Harvey must first focus his energy and identify his career goals; when he's ready, the best path to achieving them will present itself.

Comments

The need for self-awareness is stressed in this reading and Harvey would benefit from meditation and creative visualization. It is difficult for an Aries person to sit for any length of time, but the rewards could provide the incentive. Presently, his energies are scattered and his career path is directionless. The sooner Harvey gets involved with his own life, the better it will be for him.

Career Spread for Linda

Cards in the Spread

1st position	Strength (reversed)
2nd position	Knight of Pentacles (reversed)
3rd position	Four of Pentacles
4th position	The World (reversed)
5th position	Nine of Wands
6th position	The High Priestess
7th position	Three of Wands

Reading

Question 1: Is the career I have chosen what I really want?

Answer: Strength (reversed). Linda is not focused on a specific career path and is in a job she does not like. She feels she is lacking the strength to overcome her difficulties. She may feel lazy or undeserving, and have low self-esteem.

Question 2: What steps can I take to improve my career?

Answer: Knight of Pentacles (reversed). Linda needs to find a new job before she leaves her present one. She is waiting for news about money, which she will not receive. If messages do come, they will not contain news about money. The longer Linda waits, the more depressed she will become.

Question 3: Are there aspects to my career I cannot change?

Answer: Four of Pentacles. Linda is overly concerned with money—understandable when one's budget is tight. However, rather than focus on money for its own sake, she must focus on finding a job that suits her. She should understand that when you do the work that you love, the money will follow.

Question 4: Am I doing my best in my career?

Answer: The World (reversed). This card shows no success or material gain at this time. Linda knows she is not doing her best at work. She lacks vision, fears change, is frustrated, and feels she doesn't get the support she needs. Linda is a Pisces, which means her thinking may be susceptible to illusion and fantasy; she is also overly emotional.

Question 5: What changes can I make personally that will help my career?

Answer: Nine of Wands. Linda has gained knowledge through experience in her work and social life. She also knows how to protect herself in both areas of her life. She must find a job she loves, use her intelligence, and not feel as though she must always be on the defensive.

Question 6: What blocks in my past are affecting my career now?

Answer: The High Priestess. Linda desires a relationship in which she will be supported, nurtured, and cared for.

When discussing her childhood years, Linda became nervous and upset. It was simple to point out to Linda that she was still laboring under past habit patterns. She has great expectations, but she denies herself because she feels she doesn't deserve the best. Linda must forgive herself and others—this will change her life.

Question 7: Outcome?

Answer: Three of Wands. This card is associated with creative visualization and Linda should have no trouble with this; as a Pisces, the imagination is highly active. However, she must make up her mind regarding her career and the direction she wishes to go, and avoid the temptation presented by alcohol or drugs.

Comments

Linda lacks faith in her abilities and is not emotionally balanced. Although she would like to be in a relationship, she has little faith or trust in others. As a Pisces, she is extremely psychic but isn't using this talent for her own good. When she realizes that her past experiences and attitudes are creating obstacles, she can release the past, forgive herself, and find success.

LAWSUIT SPREAD

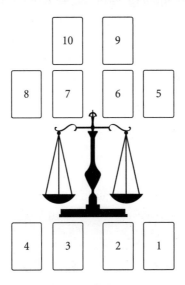

1. What is your concern regarding your case?
2. What is the conflict that is creating your insecurity?
3. Is there a fear of the opposition?
4. Are your motives honest?
5. What changes would you like to make now?
6. Is your lawyer dependable and responsible?
7. Do you visualize yourself winning the case?
8. Will there be financial rewards?
9. How long before the case is settled?
10. Final outcome?

Lawsuit Spread for Kent

Cards in the Spread

1st position	King of Pentacles
2nd position	Three of Wands
3rd position	The Fool
4th position	Seven of Swords
5th position	Ace of Cups
6th position	Seven of Cups
7th position	Judgement (reversed)
8th position	Queen of Wands
9th position	The Empress
10th position	Five of Swords

Reading

Question 1: What is your concern regarding your case?

Answer: King of Pentacles. This is a Taurus card that relates to money. Kent feels that his lawyer is competent and independent, and in control of the financial aspects of his case. He is concerned about the settlement and whether he will win the case.

Question 2: What is the conflict that is creating your insecurity?

Answer: Three of Wands. There are three lawsuits involved with this case. The court date has been postponed several times, which makes Kent nervous. He would like to see it settled and over. The Three of Wands suggests more communication is needed between Kent and his lawyer. Depression can result if Kent feels ignored and is not privy to what is happening with his case.

Question 3: Is there a fear of the opposition?

Answer: The Fool. It would be foolish of Kent not to pay attention to the opposition. Kent wants to move on to other experiences, but the dog nipping at the Fool's ankles is warning him to pay attention. The opposition is using every delaying tactic possible, and Kent must persevere and remain firm.

Question 4: Are your motives honest?

Answer: Seven of Swords. Kent feels his main goal is to clear his good name. He was wrongfully accused and feels his employer was dishonest. Kent has had his share of problems and troubles for almost two years, and they have affected his attitude in negative ways. He takes responsibility for his share of the experience and for having helped to create the situation.

Question 5: What changes would you like to make now?

Answer: Ace of Cups. New beginnings in love and emotions are on the horizon—perhaps a move to a new home, greater understanding of spiritual matters, or some intuitional guidance. Kent is eager to put the case behind him emotionally.

Question 6: Is your lawyer dependable and responsible?

Answer: Seven of Cups. Kent has faith in his lawyer and her ability to get the job done well. In his imagination, he sees himself able to do many things once she wins his case.

Question 7: Do you visualize yourself winning the case?

Answer: Judgement (reversed). Due to the last postponement, Kent has become a little unsettled. He is not paying attention to his inner self. Kent must be faithful to his vision of winning his case and not give up until he has won.

Question 8: Will there be financial rewards?

Answer: Queen of Wands. Yes. This card symbolizes money coming to Kent through his lawsuit, possibly in August. He will also get recognition and attention, and his name will be cleared.

Question 9: How long before the case is settled?

Answer: The Empress. Part of the case could be settled in October and the other part could be finished the following May. The Empress represents the creative process and infinite potential. Kent could help this process along by using creative visualization.

Question 10: Final outcome?

Answer: Five of Wands. This card shows Kent saying, "I believe in my will and my way at work or socially." Having faith in his cause is important for Kent at this time. The court will decide many factors of the case, but Kent must pay attention to his part of the drama.

Comments

Creative visualization, which Kent does regularly, seems to play a key role in this spread. Half the cards refer to other people in his life and their influence can be positive or negative. Kent must pay attention to the details and not allow himself to get distracted. Overall, the spread is positive as most of the cards are in upright positions. Since this reading, Kent has won his lawsuit and is happy.

MONEY SPREAD

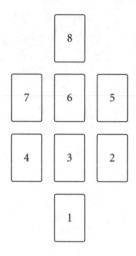

1. Concerns regarding money?
2. Desire for financial security now.
3. How can I manifest money to make me happy?
4. Past attitudes regarding money?
5. Issues regarding responsibility for financial well-being?
6. New plans for financial investments or savings?
7. What future plans am I contemplating regarding money?
8. What special abilities do I have for making money?

Money Spread for Robert

Cards in the Spread

1st position	Two of Pentacles
2nd position	The Emperor (reversed)
3rd position	Four of Wands (reversed)
4th position	Four of Pentacles (reversed)
5th position	Page of Pentacles
6th position	King of Swords (reversed)
7th position	The Lovers
8th position	Death (reversed)

Reading

Question 1: Concerns regarding money?

Answer: Two of Pentacles. Robert says he knows how to balance his money. Robert invested some money and is concerned because he has not heard good reports about his investment. He is waiting for his financial picture to change so he can be comfortable.

Question 2: Desire for financial security now.

Answer: The Emperor (reversed). In his pursuit of financial security, Robert invested in uncertain stocks. Now he is fearful and depressed over his actions. He does not realize that he is materialistic and has made money his god.

Question 3: How can I manifest money to make me happy?

Answer: Four of Wands (reversed). Robert does not realize that he is out of balance at work and in his social life.

He is not using his mind to good advantage and feels insecure. He needs to use creative visualization to bring the things he desires into his life.

Question 4: Past attitudes regarding money?

Answer: Four of Pentacles (reversed). Robert did not realize the value of money in the past. He was a spendthrift, gave money to his friends, and saved little for himself. He also had some health problems.

Question 5: Issues regarding responsibility for financial well-being?

Answer: Page of Pentacles. This Page has the desire to earn money and get ahead in his career. Robert is trying to gain his financial goals the easy way but if he is in denial, then he will lose whatever money he has invested. Robert must take responsibility for his thoughts and actions regarding money.

Question 6: New plans for financial investments or savings?

Answer: King of Swords (reversed). Robert does not have any new plans involving his finances. He is not discriminating when it concerns money and is still waiting to see if this latest investment brings him a windfall.

Question 7: What future plans am I contemplating regarding money?

Answer: The Lovers. Robert understands his past habit patterns of denial and wants to change his thinking to bring positive experiences into his life. He must learn to trust his inner self and ask for guidance. Robert has decided not to invest any more money into "get rich quick" schemes.

Question 8: What special abilities do I have for making money?

Answer: Death (reversed). The Death card is the thirteenth card of the major arcana and relates to the twelve disciples and Jesus. Perhaps this represents spiritual work in Robert's spread, as he is an astrologer with many years of study. Becoming a professional astrologer might be one way he can make money.

Comments

Robert has five cards reversed in this spread, which indicates negative thinking on his part. He needs more faith and confidence, which can be gained by accepting himself first and using his creative talents to become happy with himself and his life.

Money Spread for Peter

Cards in the Spread

1st position	King of Wands
2nd position	The Hierophant
3rd position	The Sun (reversed)
4th position	King of Cups
5th position	The Lovers (reversed)
6th position	Three of Cups
7th position	Four of Cups
8th position	Knight of Cups (reversed)

Reading

Question 1: Concerns regarding money?

Answer: King of Wands. Peter is independent, social, and enjoys entertaining his family and friends. He would like to be financially secure but is on disability pay, which limits his funds.

Question 2: Desire for financial security now.

Answer: The Hierophant. Peter longs for approval and resents any authority figure or control by others. He also resents the limitations imposed by his financial situation. Meditation may help him to get in touch with his inner guide, through which he may be able to remove any blocks relating to his need for security—be it financial, emotional, or mental.

Question 3: How can I manifest money to make me happy?

Answer: The Sun (reversed). Peter suffers from a lack of confidence in himself, yet others have great expectations for him. This can create serious health problems and family conflict. Peter must acquire a more realistic attitude about his finances.

Question 4: Past attitudes regarding money?

Answer: King of Cups. Peter is a good family man, loving and generous, but he needs to feel safe and secure. Peter tends to control his children by being overindulgent and can appear to be a spendthrift.

Question 5: Issues regarding responsibility for financial well-being?

Answer: The Lovers (reversed). Peter does not wish to make decisions about money situations, which could indicate a fear of making mistakes about them. Peter may lack trust in himself or have a closed mind about financial matters.

Question 6: New plans for financial investments or savings?

Answer: Three of Cups. Peter makes himself happy doing the things he likes best, and financial planning is not on the list. Peter prefers reading, having fun, and making plans to travel with his family. He wants to enjoy his life now rather than plan for the future.

Question 7: What future plans am I contemplating regarding money?

Answer: Four of Cups. This card reflects a person who is out of balance and unaware that something new is being offered. Peter is caught up in his old habit patterns, which must be changed for future growth.

Peter may be feeling depressed at this time because his finances don't allow for a trip or vacation. He does not feel he can change his circumstances. Perhaps this reading will cause Peter to take positive action.

Question 8: What special abilities do I have for making money?

Answer: Knight of Cups (reversed). This card shows that, although Peter is on disability, he could "make lemonade" from life's lemons by finding part-time work in a field he enjoys. Peter loves to read and he would do well working in a bookstore. Although this would take him away from his family for short periods, it could improve both his finances and his self-esteem.

Comments

There are many people involved in Peter's life, which keeps him busy. The reading reveals that Peter is a sensitive and emotional family man who would like to have more money. He must learn to take responsibility for his finances and see beyond the obvious limitations of his situation.

Money Spread for James

Cards in the Spread

1st position	Ace of Wands
2nd position	Three of Pentacles (reversed)
3rd position	The High Priestess (reversed)
4th position	Ace of Cups (reversed)
5th position	Eight of Pentacles (reversed)
6th position	Page of Swords
7th position	Eight of Cups (reversed)
8th position	Death

Reading

Question 1: Concerns regarding money?

Answer: Ace of Wands. James will have new beginnings or opportunities professionally or socially. He must incorporate some new ideas about his business in order to be successful. There is new growth potential for the business.

Question 2: Desire for financial security now.

Answer: Three of Pentacles (reversed). James does not feel his creative talents are being used to make more money. His health is good at this time but he had some major problems a short time ago. James is unhappy with one of his partners and cannot see a way to change the situation.

Question 3: How can I manifest money to make me happy?

Answer: The High Priestess (reversed). James has a fixed mental attitude regarding his business and says he doesn't know how to change his situation. He lacks trust in his intuitive abilities. To manifest anything, creative visualization is the answer. James should spend ten minutes a day focused on what he wants and have faith that it will occur.

Question 4: Past attitudes regarding money?

Answer: Ace of Cups (reversed). James feels emotionally drained. There will be no new beginnings in love, and resentment or anger can indicate a potential for health problems. James had a thriving business for thirty years, and money was not a problem. This new business takes too much time, energy, and money.

Question 5: Issues regarding responsibility for financial well-being?

Answer: Eight of Pentacles (reversed). James does not feel he has the strength to learn new skills or make money. He is very frustrated with one partner and feels that someone in the business is stealing or into criminal activities.

Question 6: New plans for financial investments or savings?

Answer: Page of Swords. James has no new financial plans except to get his business on solid ground. One partner is a young man who has his own agenda, which does not please James. Getting this man to pay attention to business would please James a lot.

Question 7: What future plans am I contemplating regarding money?

Answer: Eight of Cups (reversed). James has plans to initiate an expansion program to try to stimulate his business. He is emotionally drained and feeling unsupported. There is a lack of strength or drive, which may hamper his efforts.

Question 8: What special abilities do I have for making money?

Answer: Death. This card denotes an end to James' situation and a change for the better. He has good ideas, but feels that he is being ignored lately, which has depressed him. New ideas and future plans will be healthy. If James can release old resentments and fears, he can turn the situation around and be successful.

Comments

With so many cards reversed, it appears that James is in a negative frame of mind. His wife needs back surgery, which is not a happy event as she also works in their business. It is apparent that James and his wife are not happy due to the materialistic focus they both have.

WORK SPREAD

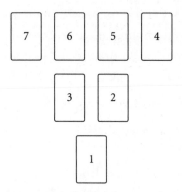

1. In what way are you concerned about your job?
2. Is the conflict beyond your control?
3. Should you communicate your feelings to your boss?
4. Is the work causing physical problems?
5. Will there be changes in the job soon?
6. Should you look for a new job?
7. Final outcome?

Work Spread for Lee

Cards in the Spread

1st position	Six of Pentacles (reversed)
2nd position	Four of Cups
3rd position	Three of Wands (reversed)
4th position	Knight of Wands
5th position	The Sun (reversed)
6th position	Seven of Cups
7th position	Two of Wands (reversed)

Reading

Question 1: In what way are you concerned about your job?

Answer: Six of Pentacles (reversed). Lee has a fear of not earning enough money and is concerned that other people make her financial choices for her. She could be a spendthrift without realizing it.

Question 2: Is the conflict beyond your control?

Answer: Four of Cups. Lee has been given a new position at work, but her salary has not yet been finalized. She has put in a lot of extra time in the last month and was informed that she will not be paid for her efforts. She can't let this depress her and throw her out of balance, causing an emotional drain and making her feel used. Unfortunately, there is nothing she can do about the situation; all she can change is her attitude.

Question 3: Should you communicate your feelings to your boss?

Answer: Three of Wands (reversed). Speaking to her boss would not be productive. Lee does not have faith in her own abilities and feels that her destiny is out of her control. She must learn to creatively visualize what she desires in her life if she wants to change her situation.

Question 4: Is the work causing physical problems?

Answer: Knight of Wands. This Knight brings information concerning work and social activities; he shows activity and energy—he is on the move. There is good news relating to work, planning a trip, or a change of residence. At this time, Lee does not have any physical problems due to her job.

Question 5: Will there be changes in the job soon?

Answer: The Sun (reversed). Lee is a teacher and her school is on a year-round calendar. She is on vacation at the time of this reading, traveling through northern California with her family. When she returns to work, she will have additional work to do as a mentor. She will need to allocate her time differently, creating changes in her daily schedule.

Question 6: Should you look for a new job?

Answer: Seven of Cups. Lee must learn to have mental control over her emotions. She loves her students and refuses to contemplate leaving them. Lee understands that nothing stays the same forever, so she will bide her time and stay where she is. Lee is a Taurus, which is a sign of patience, and she has plenty of that!

Question 7: Final outcome?

Answer: Two of Wands (reversed). Lee does not wish to take action in her work or social life if she does not have all the answers. She knows that hasty decisions may not be in her best interests. She can be too critical of herself and her abilities; this trip is providing her with breathing space.

Comments

Lee has been a teacher for about ten years and loves what she does. She is a good teacher, bilingual and creative. She is also dedicated to her students. No matter where one works, there are always problems and adjustments to be made. Lee needed to get away from all the turmoil going on at her school and this trip was ideal. Spending time with her husband and children will allow her to return to work with a more positive attitude.

Work Spread for Jeff

Cards in the Spread

1st position	The Star (reversed)
2nd position	Queen of Pentacles
3rd position	Five of Swords (reversed)
4th position	Five of Wands
5th position	The High Priestess
6th position	Six of Wands (reversed)
7th position	Seven of Swords

Reading

Question 1: In what way are you concerned about your job?

Answer: The Star (reversed). Jeff does not see any future in his job. He is the manager of his company, the highest position he can hold. Jeff must set new goals and use creative visualization to make progress in his life.

Question 2: Is the conflict beyond your control?

Answer: Queen of Pentacles. The owner of Jeff's company is very critical and judgmental. Jeff gets his share of abuse, but the owner gives it to all the help. The owner's wife tries to smooth things over and make life at work more bearable for all concerned. Jeff feels he is doing a good job and would like affirmation from his boss. Jeff has a choice—stay where he is and take the abuse, or find another job.

Question 3: Should you communicate your feelings to your boss?

Answer: Five of Swords (reversed). Jeff does not believe in creating problems and troubles. He feels no change is possible in the situation. His boss has his own ideas about running the business, and Jeff must abide by them. Jeff claims he has tried talking to his boss, but to no avail.

Question 4: Is the work causing physical problems?

Answer: Five of Wands. Yes. Jeff is having problems with his right knee (the knee relates to career and social standing). Each employee is fighting for recognition at work, and Jeff has ego needs that are not being met. These physical problems are a sign that Jeff must re-evaluate his work situation.

Question 5: Will there be changes in the job soon?

Answer: The High Priestess. Business has been up and down so much lately that Jeff says he isn't sure. But the High Priestess says he does know. Does this mean that Jeff does not want to see because he might have to make a decision?

Question 6: Should you look for a new job?

Answer: Six of Wands (reversed). This card indicates that Jeff should not make a choice at this time or someone else will make his choice for him. Success is not possible at this time but the situation could change.

Question 7: Final outcome?

Answer: Seven of Swords. The Seven of Swords means to have faith in your inner self and ask for guidance. He feels cheated in some way or believes that something is being stolen from him. A new job would no doubt be more satisfying for Jeff.

Comments

Jeff feels he is not making progress toward his goals at this time and that he must wait for a better or more clear answer. This analysis may be right at the present time, but not if Jeff continues to have physical problems related to his work that are detrimental to his well-being.

Work Spread for Joyce

Cards in the Spread

1st position	Queen of Swords
2nd position	Two of Wands
3rd position	Nine of Wands (reversed)
4th position	Nine of Swords (reversed)
5th position	Six of Pentacles
6th position	Ace of Pentacles
7th position	The Lovers

Reading

Question 1: In what way are you concerned about your job?

Answer: Queen of Swords. Joyce is a strong-willed woman and determined to make her business successful. She works very hard and desires to be a winner. She needs a back operation but feels the business is understaffed.

Question 2: Is the conflict beyond your control?

Answer: Two of Wands. Joyce knows what the conflict is in the work area and she has the control in her hands. Problems in the business have manifested a negative health situation for Joyce. She is one of three owners and each feels they know what is best for the business. Joyce must feel somewhat powerless with limited control for her back ailment to have flared up again. Back problems will occur when a person feels he or she is not getting the support he or she deserves.

Question 3: Should you communicate your feelings to your boss?

Answer: Nine of Wands (reversed). Joyce is not using the wisdom of her experiences in business and feels unprotected. There are two other owners to contend with and each has an ego that must be satisfied. The situation is not healthy and Joyce has internalized that unhealthiness.

Question 4: Is the work causing physical problems?

Answer: Nine of Swords (reversed). Yes. It is time to make changes now, as Joyce is heading toward a crisis. No time for rest and too many bosses are the factors involved in her physical problems. The work itself is not the culprit, but the mental stress Joyce is laboring under is the cause of her physical problems.

Question 5: Will there be changes in the job soon?

Answer: Six of Pentacles. Joyce must have an operation on her back. While she is gone, at least two new employees must be hired to replace her. She will have to learn to be fair and share her resources with these new people. While she is off work, Joyce could visualize different ways to make money.

Question 6: Should you look for a new job?

Answer: Ace of Pentacles. Since Joyce owns a share of the business, she is not interested in a "job." However, this card shows new beginnings in money and prosperity and speaks of better health for Joyce. One of her business partners is her husband and she must understand that their relationship is based on financial security. They are enlarging their workplace and this card indicates that doing so is a successful move.

Question 7: Final outcome?

Answer: The Lovers. Joyce must choose what to do with her life. She must use discrimination, be responsible, and have faith that she will make good decisions. Whatever Joyce decides, it will affect her husband and her own family. Removing herself from the combat zone will not solve the problems, only postpone them. She must decide.

Comments

The three bosses of this business are related to each other, and all of them seem to have short fuses. To heal their relationship, it would be wise to sell the business. It seems this is not possible at this time, although the problems are mounting. Getting more help, which would allow Joyce to spend less time working, may defuse the situation.

LEGAL MATTERS 2 SPREAD

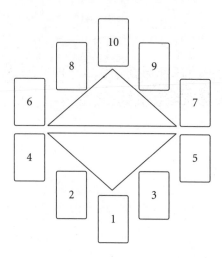

1. What is your concern regarding the legal matter?
2. What is your mental state about this experience?
3. What steps are you taking while you wait for results?
4. Is there a reason for delays or obstacles?
5. How do you feel about your legal counsel?
6. How do you relate to the other person's lawyer?
7. Do you have reliable witnesses?
8. Is your financial position stable?
9. Do you feel supported by your friends and family?
10. Final outcome?

Five

Life's
Big Decisions

This group of four spreads concerns some of life's biggest and most important issues. The spreads are:

Relationship Problems

Marriage

Pregnancy

Divorce Potential

These matters cannot be taken lightly and the reader must be aware of the serious nature of the topic. In many cases, the querent believes that the reader is omnipotent and can see the answer to his or her dilemma. As always, be truthful and end the reading on an upbeat note as much as possible.

The last spread in this chapter is Divorce Potential and does not have a sample reading. At the time of this writing, no one came forward with this desire in mind.

The questions in all of the spreads are direct. Each person must look within to find true answers to the questions posed. The tarot cards have the ability to help individuals resolve their problems if the querent will allow the truth to shine forth.

RELATIONSHIP PROBLEMS

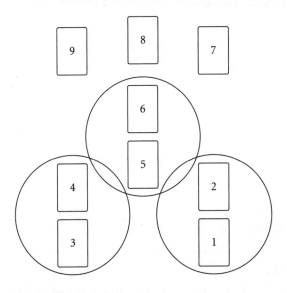

1. What is the problem?
2. What is the conflict?
3. Did I create the problem?
4. Am I refusing to see my part of the problem?
5. Past experiences with my partner?
6. Are we abusive to each other?
7. Are other people involved with our problem?
8. Are there financial problems affecting our relationship?
9. Will this relationship end?

Relationship Problems for Joanie

Cards in the Spread

1st position	Queen of Pentacles (reversed)
2nd position	King of Wands
3rd position	Seven of Wands (reversed)
4th position	Six of Swords
5th position	Three of Swords (reversed)
6th position	The Hanged Man
7th position	Six of Wands (reversed)
8th position	Ten of Swords
9th position	Page of Wands

Reading

Question 1: What is the problem?

Answer: Queen of Pentacles (reversed). Joanie is a spend-thrift and would prefer not to work. She wants to be taken care of and has not found a person who will support her in the style she wishes.

Question 2: What is the conflict?

Answer: King of Wands. Joanie has many Aries traits. She wants everything now. She is ambitious and independent, with executive talents and leadership qualities. Her conflict is in bringing a similar type of male into her life—someone who wants her to take care of him and support him. This is very frustrating for her.

Question 3: Did I create the problem?

Answer: Seven of Wands (reversed). Joanie has an inferiority complex and may feel incompetent, attitudes that can undermine any relationship. Joanie also has a physical and material focus, which is not a sound basis for a healthy emotional relationship. She does not drink, smoke, or indulge in drugs and will not tolerate anyone who does. Due to Joanie's ego needs, if she does not get attention, she will end the affair. She understands that she creates her own reality, but is determined to find that special person who will fulfill her dreams.

Question 4: Am I refusing to see my part of the problem?

Answer: Six of Swords. Joanie has been tempted to run away from her problems, but she understands that she must stay and work things out in order to advance in life. Joanie had problems with her father when she was a child, and this has colored all her relationships with men. She has begun reading self-help books and wants to understand her part in the situation.

Question 5: Past experiences with my partner?

Answer: Three of Swords (reversed). In the past, Joanie believed that she did not create her own problems. She was unhappily married and finally divorced her husband, and has not had a long-term relationship since then. Joanie does not respect men due to her negative experiences with her father.

Question 6: Are we abusive to each other?

Answer: The Hanged Man. Up to this point, Joanie feels that she has been sacrificed to the will of others. She feels in bondage; that no matter what the issue, she will not win. Fantasy and illusion cloud her reasoning and some of her ideas are without substance. Joanie wants something from her relationships but she must learn to let go—in this way, she frees herself. No one can abuse her if she won't let them.

Question 7: Are other people involved with our problem?

Answer: Six of Wands (reversed). Joanie has siblings and other relatives with whom she is involved. Her dad died recently and she is caught up in an inheritance battle. At this time, she wants what she can get from the estate—it may finally resolve her negative feelings about her father so she can get on with her life.

Question 8: Are there financial problems affecting our relationship?

Answer: Ten of Swords. Joanie did not have pressing financial difficulties in her last relationship, but there were emotional ones that undermined it. For Joanie, there will be major changes in her problems when she receives her inheritance. Many burdens will be lifted and some of her more serious issues will be taken care of. A new cycle is beginning for her, which can affect her emotionally and bring happier times.

Question 9: Will this relationship end?

Answer: Page of Wands. This Page desires freedom—so does Joanie. She was not in a relationship at the time of the reading and will probably not have a serious relationship for some time to come.

Comments

Joanie is studying spiritual work in earnest and is now more aware of her attitudes and how they worked against her in past relationships. She vows to do things differently in the future.

Relationship Problems for Ann

Cards in the Spread

1st position	Three of Cups (reversed)
2nd position	Two of Swords
3rd position	Seven of Wands
4th position	Eight of Pentacles
5th position	Queen of Cups
6th position	The Emperor (reversed)
7th position	Six of Cups
8th position	The Sun
9th position	Five of Cups (reversed)

Reading

Question 1: What is the problem?

Answer: Three of Cups (reversed). Ann feels she is having an emotional crisis. She is having problems in her personal relationships and there is depression, unhappiness, and a lack of creativity in her life.

Question 2: What is the conflict?

Answer: Two of Swords. Ann doesn't want to see her problems and troubles. She must meditate to find answers.

Ann may need to take action instead of waiting passively for the situation to clear up.

Question 3: Did I create the problem?

Answer: Seven of Wands. Ann should understand that we create our own reality. She needs to take responsibility, avoid feeling superior, and use her ego and will in positive ways. This path can lead to success both professionally and in her relationships.

Question 4: Am I refusing to see my part of the problem?

Answer: Eight of Pentacles. When we are involved in difficulties, it is often impossible to see solutions. However, by persevering in learning new skills and having the strength to cope with all types of experiences, Ann will see that everything ties together.

Question 5: Past experiences with my partner?

Answer: Queen of Cups. This Queen is a Scorpio and associated with love and emotions. Ann is powerful, intuitive, and intense. She is a good friend and a dangerous enemy. Although her husband is deceased, she continues to work and stay busy.

Question 6: Are we abusive to each other?

Answer: The Emperor (reversed). Ann does not realize her potential. She must learn to follow through with her plans, not be lazy or fearful. She must accept the fact that she has to rely on herself and her inner source for guidance.

Question 7: Are other people involved with our problem?

Answer: Six of Cups. This card refers to choices Ann must make regarding love and emotions. She will be tempted to live in the past, but the present has the potential to be a happier place for her. There are new responsibilities and a potential new relationship.

Question 8: Are there financial problems affecting our relationship?

Answer: The Sun. Ann is seeking truth and happiness. There is a potential for financial gain, a trip, and an increase in self-confidence. There are certain limitations, but this card shows no material loss. Health and abundance are assured.

Question 9: Will this relationship end?

Answer: Five of Cups (reversed). Ann is still emotionally drained over the loss of her husband. There is some fear of the future and she has lost faith in love or romance. If there has been a relationship since her loss, it was very brief.

Comments

Ann is still young enough to get involved in a fulfilling relationship. Companionship is the answer for senior citizens and can give new direction and meaning to life. Now is the time to take a chance.

MARRIAGE SPREAD

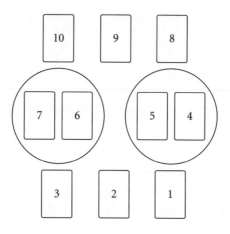

1. Will I ever marry?
2. What kind of mate is compatible?
3. Will we have good methods of communication?
4. Will we both desire a commitment?
5. Will we have similar likes and dislikes?
6. Will this person's family accept me?
7. How shall we find each other?
8. Will we be able to share our financial resources?
9. What can I do while I am waiting for my mate?
10. Outcome?

Marriage Spread for Laura

Cards in the Spread

1st position	The Tower (reversed)
2nd position	Temperance (reversed)
3rd position	Queen of Swords (reversed)
4th position	Five of Wands
5th position	Queen of Pentacles (reversed)
6th position	Four of Swords
7th position	Page of Swords
8th position	The Wheel of Fortune
9th position	Four of Pentacles (reversed)
10th position	King of Swords (reversed)

Reading

Question 1: Will I ever marry?

Answer: The Tower (reversed). Laura is afraid to change her old thought patterns concerning marriage. She fears losing her freedom; she has had one failed marriage and does not wish to repeat the experience. However, there is presently potential for a new marriage.

Question 2: What kind of mate is compatible?

Answer: Temperance (reversed). This card shows an imbalance in Laura's emotional life. She is a Gemini and this card represents Sagittarius, her opposite sign. Sagittarius is a freedom lover, one who desires to travel and meet all kinds of people. This would be an ideal situation, although the men Laura has been involved with lately are of the dominant type. Laura admitted that she was afraid of being hurt in love.

Question 3: Will we have good methods of communication?

Answer: Queen of Swords (reversed). Laura is not open and honest with herself. She would like to be married but fears making a mistake. Laura must communicate this to her new love if she intends to build a lasting relationship.

Question 4: Will we both desire a commitment?

Answer: Five of Wands. This card relates to strife and disharmony. Laura is independent and may decide not to get involved with anyone. She may have a difficult time committing herself at this time. She believes in her own ideas and has the will to see them through, but she believes she must fight to get her ego needs met.

Question 5: Will we have similar likes and dislikes?

Answer: Queen of Pentacles (reversed). Laura and her new love have spoken of marriage and children. Laura is not interested in having children and this factor makes her more fearful. She wants to enjoy her life and be free to travel. She and her new love have similar desires, but not in regard to children.

Question 6: Will this person's family accept me?

Answer: Four of Swords. This card shows an imbalance in Laura's emotional life. Her new love comes from a wealthy family from the East Coast and she feels a little uncertain about being welcomed into this family.

Question 7: How shall we find each other?

Answer: Page of Swords. Laura and her new love have found each other and they must stop paying attention to others. Listening to her heart's desire will show Laura the way to happiness. Only Laura knows what is best for herself—listening to others can confuse the issue. She can be childish with her fears of losing her freedom by getting married.

Question 8: Will we be able to share our financial resources?

Answer: The Wheel of Fortune. The Wheel of Fortune says "take a chance, gamble, and travel." Her new love has money of his own and their financial picture looks very bright.

Question 9: What can I do while I am waiting for my mate?

Answer: Four of Pentacles (reversed). Laura must create balance in her finances and health. Money is not the most important issue here. Laura must realize that this could be her magical dream come true and go for it.

Question 10: Outcome?

Answer: King of Swords (reversed). This reversed King is fickle and superficial. He is also a Gemini, like Laura. This indicates that the outcome is up to Laura and that her future is in her hands.

Comments

With many cards reversed in this spread, it is apparent that Laura is not thinking clearly. She will have to make a decision, but she has time. This new relationship can work out if there is love between the two parties. Only they know the truth!

Marriage Spread for Glenda

Cards in the Spread

1st position	Knight of Pentacles
2nd position	Five of Wands
3rd position	Page of Wands
4th position	The Hanged Man (reversed)
5th position	Four of Wands (reversed)
6th position	The Wheel of Fortune (reversed)
7th position	The Hermit
8th position	King of Swords
9th position	Four of Cups
10th position	Queen of Swords (reversed)

Reading

Question 1: Will I ever marry?

Answer: Knight of Pentacles. Glenda wants to marry if she finds a man of means who can support them both. She is waiting for an opportunity to go on vacation with him if he is willing to pay the bills.

Question 2: What kind of mate is compatible?

Answer: Five of Wands. This card refers to a belief that one must fight to get one's ideas across at work and socially. With faith, one does not need to fight aggressively. Glenda wants a mate who will seek higher goals, use his will to gain recognition, and make money. Glenda's beliefs will bring her success if she is thinking positively.

Question 3: Will we have good methods of communication?

Answer: Page of Wands. This card shows an immature person who wants to work and have an active social life. Glenda and her gentleman friend have little time together; he travels a good deal and stays busy.

Question 4: Will we both desire a commitment?

Answer: The Hanged Man (reversed). Glenda must be realistic and not just "hang in there" hoping things will change. She should meditate on this relationship to see if it is positive or futile. Perhaps she is committed, but he is not.

Question 5: Will we have similar likes and dislikes?

Answer: Four of Wands (reversed): Glenda does not realize her thinking is out of balance. This card reversed shows no marriage, a lack of stability, and an unfruitful relationship. Glenda and her friend may have similar likes and dislikes, but no basis for marriage.

Question 6: Will this person's family accept me?

Answer: The Wheel of Fortune (reversed). This is not the time for Glenda to gamble that his family will accept her. She must first build a relationship. Her friend is divorced and has two daughters, which could also present problems.

Question 7: How shall we find each other?

Answer: The Hermit. Glenda has been divorced and has gained wisdom through her experiences. She must get in touch with her inner source and find the light to guide her to a loving partner.

Question 8: Will we be able to share our financial resources?

Answer: King of Swords. This is the card of a lawyer. Glenda may feel that she will need to protect herself legally or sign a prenuptial agreement in the event she does marry. This card advises caution—she should think about her financial expectations.

Question 9: What can I do while I am waiting for my mate?

Answer: Four of Cups. Glenda must realize that she is still holding on to her past love affairs (or her marriage). She needs to look at what is coming her way now—a new beginning in love—and grab it! Glenda must balance her emotions rather than being ruled by them. By changing her beliefs, she will change her life.

Question 10: Outcome?

Answer: Queen of Swords (reversed). Glenda does not want to stay single—she wants a marriage with equality and balance. She has problems and troubles of her own but Glenda would feel better about herself if she were married. She desires a mate—and soon!

Comments

Glenda must give up her past attitudes about men in order to have a positive relationship. She must not seek "unavailable" men and then hope to change them. If she feels this man is immature, why desire the relationship to continue? Glenda is a Virgo and perhaps more critical and judgmental than she realizes, especially about men.

PREGNANCY SPREAD

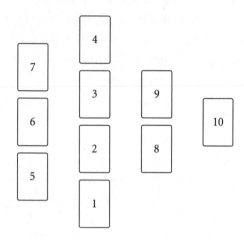

1. Am I ready for a child?
2. Do I have enough confidence to be a parent?
3. Will I be happy being a parent?
4. Will the other parent be supportive of the child?
5. Will I feel trapped or a lack of freedom because of the child?
6. What past behavior do I need to change to be better prepared for parenting?
7. Will I be able to give this child a good education?
8. Is there potential for the child to have health problems?
9. Will my parents be involved and supportive?
10. Final outcome?

Pregnancy Spread for Marcie

Cards in the Spread

1st position	Eight of Pentacles (reversed)
2nd position	The High Priestess (reversed)
3rd position	Eight of Wands (reversed)
4th position	Three of Pentacles (reversed)
5th position	The Empress (reversed)
6th position	Six of Swords
7th position	Queen of Cups (reversed)
8th position	Ten of Cups
9th position	The Wheel of Fortune
10th position	The Fool (reversed)

Reading

Question 1: Am I ready for a child?

Answer: Eight of Pentacles (reversed). Marcie lacks confidence in herself and feels she does not have the strength to have a child now. She is divorced and has never had children of her own. She also wants quick money but does not wish to work hard to get it. Marcie's new partner has money but there are conditions she may not be willing to accept.

Question 2: Do I have enough confidence to be a parent?

Answer: The High Priestess (reversed). Marcie does not know if she would make a good parent. She has some fixed ideas and tends to overanalyze her experiences. She is having an emotionally draining period trying to make important decisions.

Question 3: Will I be happy being a parent?

Answer: Eight of Wands (reversed). Marcie lacks strength in her work and social activities. She feels vulnerable and insecure. Her thoughts are unbalanced and could lead to the end of her new relationship. She is definitely not committed to becoming a parent, so happiness is not the issue for her now.

Question 4: Will the other parent be supportive of the child?

Answer: Three of Pentacles (reversed). Marcie has little faith or trust in her creative abilities, which would include bringing a child into the world. However, her new love has money and the potential to inherit more, so he would be financially able to support a child.

Question 5: Will I feel trapped or a lack of freedom because of the child?

Answer: The Empress (reversed). Marcie has problems with her mother and other women. She has a fear of losing her freedom and feels sexually unfulfilled, so she may not commit to a relationship now. The relationship may be over before it really starts. Without a relationship, she would not want a child.

Question 6: What past behavior do I need to change to be better prepared for parenting?

Answer: Six of Swords (reversed). Marcie has no choice about making changes—she must stay and face the issues and work them out. Marcie finds it difficult to make decisions, especially about having children.

Question 7: Will I be able to give this child a good education?

Answer: Queen of Cups (reversed). Yes, if she marries this new love who has plenty of money and is a professional in his career. But Marcie is not being honest with this man—she is emotionally drained, resentful, and afraid to trust her heart.

Question 8: Is there a potential for the child to have health problems?

Answer: Ten of Cups. Marcie does not need to worry about the child's health. This card refers to love on a higher plane and, with the rainbow, some good luck. The scene is happy and healthy for the entire family.

Question 9: Will my parents be involved and supportive?

Answer: The Wheel of Fortune. Most parents welcome grandchildren and are supportive in many ways. Marcie must take a chance on her life. She must let go of old ties in her personal life that have become a burden. It is time for new experiences and taking risks. The time is right for success!

Question 10: Final outcome?

Answer: The Fool (reversed). Marcie is not really looking for new experiences of a lasting nature. She is lacking confidence, and is sexually focused and materialistic. Marcie needs to balance her pleasures, desires, and sexual attitudes with a more spiritual outlook, and have faith in the future.

Comments

Marcie is fearful of making another error in judgment. She has had a failed marriage and does not want to repeat that experience. She confessed her need for freedom and the opportunity to get casually involved whenever she felt like it. Until she changes her focus, a lasting relationship— let alone a child—is out of reach for her.

Pregnancy Spread for Betty

Cards in the Spread

1st position	The Sun (reversed)
2nd position	Six of Cups
3rd position	Queen of Wands (reversed)
4th position	Ten of Wands
5th position	Knight of Cups (reversed)
6th position	Ace of Swords (reversed)
7th position	Ten of Swords
8th position	Nine of Cups
9th position	Death
10th position	Eight of Swords

Reading

Question 1: Am I ready for a child?

Answer: The Sun (reversed). Betty lacks courage and confidence at this time, which means she should not have a child now. Her low energy may be detrimental to herself and the child and lead to health problems in the future. Betty has been disappointed in her relationships and this may be one of the reasons she is not ready to commit to becoming a mother.

Question 2: Do I have enough confidence to be a parent?

Answer: Six of Cups. This card shows the tendency to live in the past, or to bring someone from the past into her life again, and that may not be positive. Betty is divorced, but she does not want to be a single parent. She is waiting for the right man to ask that important question, then she may consider having a child.

Question 3: Will I be happy being a parent?

Answer: Queen of Wands (reversed). This Queen is a Leo, and people of this sign usually love children. They have great expectations and want their children to do well, as it is a reflection on the Leo ego. However, Betty is career-minded, so having a child may be a barrier to her ambitions.

Question 4: Will the other parent be supportive of the child?

Answer: Ten of Wands. According to this card the answer is yes. Betty would not have to carry the burden alone and her job could get better along the way. The other parent will help Betty in many ways in addition to supporting the child.

Question 5: Will I feel trapped or a lack of freedom because of the child?

Answer: Knight of Cups (reversed). Lack of freedom is Betty's greatest fear. Just thinking about having a child has created an emotional drain and stress in her relationship. The Knight indicates that she did not get the message she was expecting and now she prefers not to make any decisions. Betty may be a procrastinator and not always honest.

Question 6: What past behavior do I need to change to be better prepared for parenting?

Answer: Ace of Swords (reversed). Betty must change some of her negative beliefs. Meditation and creative visualization can help her do this. She has little self-confidence or self-esteem, something that must be dealt with and resolved. All first-time parents feel a great deal of stress and want to do a good job raising their children, but experience is the only teacher when dealing with babies.

Question 7: Will I be able to give this child a good education?

Answer: Ten of Swords. This card indicates major changes are in store for Betty. Burdens will be lifted and her negative cycle is passing. There is plenty of time to be concerned with a complete education for a child who is not born yet.

Question 8: Is there a potential for the child to have health problems?

Answer: Nine of Cups. The "wish card" upright means the querent will get his or her wish. As Betty was thinking about health matters in regard to the child, I would say that the child would be in excellent health.

Question 9: Will my parents be involved and supportive?

Answer: Death. Betty's father is dead but her mother is alive and well and will be supportive, accepting the child under any circumstances. This child would symbolize an end to an old way of life and a change for the better. This is the time for transformation, so I advised Betty to let go of old experiences that have no meaning in her life now and grab new opportunities.

Question 10: Final outcome?

Answer: Eight of Swords. Betty has the strength to cope with all her experiences, and especially with her problems. She has a fear of making changes or taking risks. This can be a frustrating time for her, but only she can make the final decisions.

Comments

It is difficult to raise a child as a single parent, but many do so. Betty is in her forties and will soon run out of time to give birth to a child of her own. Feeling she has made a previous mistake in marriage, she is reluctant to try again. These decisions are very personal and Betty is the only one capable of making them for herself. She is still weighing her options.

DIVORCE POTENTIAL

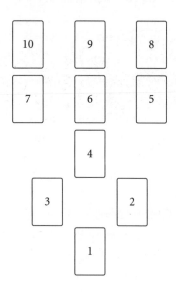

1. What reasons do I have for wanting a divorce?
2. Do I still love my mate?
3. Are we cheating each other or on each other?
4. Is money our problem? Do we use it as a tool against each other?
5. Are we still sexually compatible?
6. Why won't my mate accept more responsibility?
7. Does my mate have problems with alcohol or drugs?
8. Do we try to control and abuse each other?
9. Can I change my negative feelings about my marriage?
10. Final outcome?

Six

On the Move

In this chapter, travel and making changes are high-lighted. There are four spreads, three with sample readings and one without. The spreads are:

Desire to Move

Taking a Trip

Relocation

Planning a Trip

The last spread, Planning a Trip, uses only six cards and should provide enough information in the reading to satisfy the querent. Each spread relates to changes of some kind for the individual and will supply information to help him or her make choices.

Once an idea has been planted in a person's mind, it must be thought over until a conclusion is reached. New ideas that propel us forward are always healthy. They lift us out of our ruts and into a new realm of hope and curiosity.

Looking forward to a new adventure can be very stimulating and the tarot cards help us to identify all the good things the universe has to offer.

DESIRE TO MOVE

10	9	8
6		7
4		5
3	2	1

1. What are my concerns involving this move?
2. What is the conflict?
3. Will I be happy when I make this move?
4. How will my new home, new area, and work affect me?
5. What are my options about the move in the next few weeks?
6. What choices did I make in the past that are affecting me now?
7. Will I learn new skills at work or at home?
8. What does my financial future hold for me?
9. What are my hopes and fears about the move?
10. Final outcome?

Desire to Move for Andrea

Cards in the Spread

1st position	Two of Pentacles (reversed)
2nd position	Four of Pentacles
3rd position	Seven of Cups
4th position	Nine of Pentacles (reversed)
5th position	The Lovers
6th position	Four of Cups (reversed)
7th position	The High Priestess
8th position	Ace of Pentacles
9th position	Eight of Wands (reversed)
10th position	Page of Pentacles (reversed)

Reading

Question I: What are my concerns involving this move?

Answer: Two of Pentacles (reversed). Andrea is a free spender and does not like to budget her money. She fears the move will be expensive and is rather reluctant since she has only been in her present place for two years.

Question 2: What is the conflict?

Answer: Four of Pentacles. Andrea, a senior citizen, does not know whether to rent or buy. Her conflict is trying to rent a nice place inexpensively. Andrea would like to hold on to her resources for security reasons. She also owns property that she has rented to others. Her mixed feelings are contributing to her feeling "stuck."

Question 3: Will I be happy when I make this move?

Answer: Seven of Cups. This move could be the path to happiness! If Andrea surrounds herself with positive thoughts, she will find the perfect place. Creative visualization can create an environment that makes all one's dreams come true.

Question 4: How will my new home, new area, and work affect me?

Answer: Nine of Pentacles (reversed). Andrea is not using wisdom in her finances. She has been a widow for several years and is still learning through experience about money matters. Andrea does not feel independent or able to do things on her own, but she is learning.

Question 5: What are my options about the move in the next few weeks?

Answer: The Lovers. Andrea has the choice of staying where she is or moving back to the area in which she used to live. She presently is living close to her son, his wife, and Andrea's two grandchildren.

Question 4: What choices did I make in the past that are affecting me now?

Answer: Four of Cups (reversed). Thinking about leaving her two grandchildren leaves Andrea emotionally drained. She admitted that her help with the children was not being utilized by her daughter-in-law, and that had been the reason she moved near the family. The decision Andrea made in the past was not a positive one for her.

Question 7: Will I learn new skills at work or home?

Answer: The High Priestess. Andrea is smart and she knows a lot that she could share with others, given the opportunity. It will be a happier experience for Andrea to be back among her old friends.

Question 8: What does my financial future hold for me?

Answer: Ace of Pentacles. It appears that Andrea will have new beginnings with money, probably as a result of the move.

Question 9: What are my hopes and fears about the move?

Answer: Eight of Wands (reversed). Andrea feels a lack of strength in dealing with her son's family. They did not interact socially and Andrea felt rebuffed at other contact with her daughter-in-law. Andrea fears she will not have much contact with this family if she moves. She hopes for the best for them, but she also hopes for a happier situation for herself.

Question 10: Final outcome?

Answer: Page of Pentacles (reversed). This card refers to the student who refuses to make money for schooling. The Page is an earth sign, practical and material. Andrea's two young grandchildren are both Taurus, and one will be entering school in September.

Comments

Regardless of what happens in her son's life, Andrea must make her decisions based on what is best for her. She can stay in touch with her grandchildren even if she doesn't live nearby. This spread has shown a great deal of thinking about money, which is not healthy. Andrea needs other interests to keep herself happy and involved with living her life to her fullest potential.

Desire to Move for Sylvia

Cards in the Spread

1st position	Justice (reversed)
2nd position	The Hermit
3rd position	Page of Pentacles
4th position	Seven of Cups (reversed)
5th position	Two of Cups (reversed)
6th position	Nine of Wands (reversed)
7th position	Temperance
8th position	Knight of Wands
9th position	Five of Wands (reversed)
10th position	The Wheel of Fortune

Reading

Question 1: What are my concerns involving this move?

Answer: Justice (reversed). There could be legal problems and Sylvia's health could be affected. She feels her landlord is very unfair and she has had problems with other landlords; she dreads getting involved with a new one. Sylvia prefers owning her own home and has negative feelings about renting.

Question 2: What is the conflict?

Answer: The Hermit. This card reflects an ending to some situation that has been handled in a positive manner. Sylvia must remember her past landlords, bless them, and release them. If she holds onto her negative feelings about them, the lesson will be repeated. Using wisdom gained through experience brings success.

Question 3: Will I be happy when I make this move?

Answer: Page of Pentacles. This is the card of the student who is interested in making money, having a career, and reaching the top in his or her chosen field. Sylvia is ambitious, materialistic, and somewhat traditional. She sees greater opportunities for her career by making a move, as well as a chance to find happiness in a new area.

Question 4: How will my new home, new area, and work affect me?

Answer: Seven of Cups (reversed). This card reversed does not assure success for Sylvia. There could be a loss through love or an emotional drain due to the move. Sylvia needs to do creative visualization and bring positive experiences into her life. She also needs more faith and trust in her inner resources.

Question 5: What are my options about the move in the next few weeks?

Answer: Two of Cups (reversed). Sylvia is uncertain about her direction and there are no easy answers to her ques-

tions. Perhaps the move will take longer than she antici-
pated or her health will be affected by stress.

Question 6: What choices did I make in the past that are affecting me now?

Answer: Nine of Wands (reversed). This card reversed
refers to delayed plans and a lack of wisdom gained
through experience. Sylvia was not open to new information in the past and may have been intolerant, critical,
and judgmental. Some of the choices she made were not
as positive as she thought.

Question 7: Will I learn new skills at work or at home?

Answer: Temperance. Sylvia has the potential to find positive outlets for her energy, learn self-control, and achieve
harmony within herself. She could also learn to have more
patience and temper her ego needs. She will have the opportunity to learn new skills in the near future, but her
most important work will be on herself.

Question 8: What does my financial future hold for me?

Answer: Knight of Wands. This messenger is bringing
Sylvia good news relating to work, planning a trip, or a
change of residence. Sylvia has the potential for a bright
future and financial well-being.

Question 9: What are my hopes and fears about the move?

Answer: Five of Wands (reversed). Sylvia's fears are focused on work and her social life. These fears may be

preventing her from moving. She does not desire to fight for her ideas and suffers from a lack of self-confidence. Sylvia must use creative visualization about her business and believe that her inner source will guide her in the right direction.

Question 10: Final outcome?

Answer: The Wheel of Fortune. This card indicates it is time to make changes, take a chance on a new venture, or travel. Gambling for fun or profit is also favored now. This would be a good time for Sylvia to make herself happy. The success that Sylvia is seeking is there for her—but she needs a positive attitude and the desire to win!

Comments

There are many people involved with Sylvia in her business and in her life (there are four major arcana cards and two court cards, all telling of people affecting the querent). Sylvia is interested in change and her life has been full of it. Looking back at her experiences, she sees that she has been successful in many areas of her life and that it need not change now. In the end, Sylvia is the one who must make the decision to move, thus setting new events in motion.

TAKING A TRIP

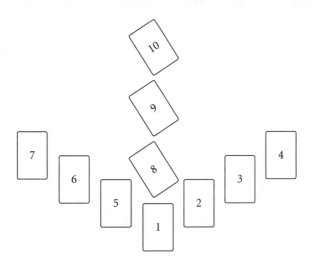

1. Where do I want to go?
2. Do I have enough money for a trip?
3. Should I go with friends or family?
4. Would I be happier on a tour?
5. Shall I go by plane?
6. Shall I go by boat or train?
7. What are the obstacles to my trip?
8. What kind of experiences will I have?
9. Will I meet someone special on this trip?
10. Outcome?

Taking a Trip for Tara

Cards in the Spread

1st position	Knight of Wands (reversed)
2nd position	The High Priestess
3rd position	The Fool (reversed)
4th position	Page of Wands
5th position	Two of Swords (reversed)
6th position	Six of Pentacles (reversed)
7th position	Queen of Swords
8th position	Nine of Swords (reversed)
9th position	Five of Cups (reversed)
10th position	Four of Swords (reversed)

Reading

Question 1: Where do I want to go?

Answer: Knight of Wands (reversed). This Knight brings negative news regarding work and social activities, which may indicate delays and frustration at work and socially. Tara and several of her friends were planning a cruise ship tour, but two of them have been fighting. They all want to back out, but Tara had her heart set on this trip. She is upset and angry over the turn of events.

Question 2: Do I have enough money for a trip?

Answer: The High Priestess. Tara can afford this trip. She also has enough money to board her dog, whom she loves dearly, although she is not sure she wants to leave him.

Question 3: Should I go with friends or family?

Answer: The Fool (reversed). Tara needs more confidence and must take responsibility for making her own decisions. Her friends are acting immaturely and will miss out if they don't go. Tara has waited a long time for this trip and would be foolish to give it up.

Question 4: Would I be happier on a tour?

Answer: Page of Wands. This Page is eager to experience life and to be out in public. Tara needs change, new experiences, and excitement in her life, as she rarely goes anywhere. She really wants to go on this cruise, which is a tour of several Caribbean islands.

Question 5: Shall I go by plane?

Answer: Two of Swords (reversed). Tara does not want to fly. She's never flown before and has a fear of flying. However, a cruise is ideal for her. It is a leisurely way to travel with all accommodations and food included.

Question 6: Shall I go by boat or train?

Answer: Six of Pentacles (reversed). This vacation is already planned and a ship is the method of travel. Tara did agree to go and she can afford it, though she may fear losing her deposit. If her friends don't stop feuding, she may not go at all.

Question 7: What are the obstacles to my trip?

Answer: Queen of Swords. This card refers to a Libra woman—Tara is a Libra. Libras often have problems making decisions, fearing they are not right. This means that she creates her own obstacles and is hesitant to spend money on pleasure trips. Tara is used to having to deal with problems and rarely takes time to indulge herself.

Question 8: What kind of experiences will I have?

Answer: Nine of Swords (reversed). Tara fears she will not enjoy herself on this trip. She is not in crisis, but she could create her own drama due to her insecurities, low self-esteem, or indecision (a Libra trait).

Question 9: Will I meet someone special on this trip?

Answer: Five of Cups (reversed). This card indicates that Tara refuses to believe in love or romance. She feels emotionally drained by family matters, including the loss of her parents. Tara is holding onto past relationships and feels she has passed her prime. She is a loner, but still young enough to have a good relationship if she wants it.

Question 10: Outcome?

Answer: Four of Swords (reversed). Tara does not recognize her problems and troubles. She is doing too much; she just got transferred on her job, and now this problem of "are we going or not?" has arisen. As of the time of this writing, no decisions had been made and the trip is in limbo.

Comments

It has been a long time since Tara has done something nice for herself. After the reading, she was almost convinced that she should go. One of her friends said she would go if Tara wanted to. Of course, it is always more fun to have a group, but if that doesn't work, why not go anyway? However, considering all the reversed cards in this spread, the trip will probably not take place.

Taking a Trip for Jody

Cards in the Spread

1st position	Ace of Swords
2nd position	The Lovers
3rd position	The Moon
4th position	Four of Wands
5th position	Queen of Pentacles
6th position	The Devil (reversed)
7th position	Three of Swords
8th position	Ten of Cups
9th position	The Hierophant
10th position	Death

Reading

Question 1: Where do I want to go?

Answer: Ace of Swords. Jody has been thinking about taking a vacation but is not sure where she would like to go. She feels there are new problems for her to resolve in her personal life and taking a trip might not be possible.

Question 2: Do I have enough money for a trip?

Answer: The Lovers. Jody must make decisions in her life. By accepting her responsibilities and having faith in her inner source, she will realize her abundance. Now is the time for a trip or other happy events. This card is also a warning that Jody should take care of health needs now.

Question 3: Should I go with friends or family?

Answer: The Moon. Jody has all kinds of fears and she must decide if she will be more comfortable among friends or family. Jody is ruled by her emotions and often ends up feeling victimized. She does not always want to see the truth, and some of her friends are not loyal.

Question 4: Would I be happier on a tour?

Answer: Four of Wands. This card relates to marriage, work, and social activities. Perhaps Jody would consider a tour where she could meet other people. She must realize it is her right to choose where to go and with whom. The good news is that, if she decides to take a tour, she will greatly enjoy it.

Question 5: Shall I go by plane?

Answer: Queen of Pentacles. Jody works hard to make money and spending it is difficult for her. She is an idealist and a perfectionist, so all the details will be worked out first. Her decision whether to go by plane will be determined by cost.

Question 6: Shall I go by boat or train?

Answer: The Devil (reversed). Jody does have a preference. She wants to take a trip but she does not want to spend a lot of money. A cruise ship would be Jody's first choice, if the price is not exorbitant.

Question 7: What are the obstacles to my trip?

Answer: Three of Swords. Jody must understand that she is creating her own problems. Her siblings want to take the trip with her, but they can't agree on the time. Her decision must be based on her own needs or she may miss the opportunity to go at all. Jody feels defensive, as if some members of her family are trying to cheat her out of her vacation.

Question 8: What kind of experiences will I have?

Answer: Ten of Cups. Jody will have positive changes in her love and emotional life due to this trip, which is definitely slated for her at this time. There could be a new relationship, and the vacation could even help heal tense relations between Jody and her siblings.

Question 9: Will I meet someone special on this trip?

Answer: The Hierophant. There is the potential for Jody to learn a great deal on this trip. It may be through her inner source or through someone she gets involved with. It will be a time to meditate and trust her intuition.

Question 10: Outcome?

Answer: Death. Past situations are ending now and Jody has new ideas and plans for the future, which indicate a change for the better. She must be open to love, let go of old habit patterns, and release resentments. She can use her energy to manifest a richer and fuller life.

Comments

Getting rid of old habit patterns is an important matter for everyone. Meditation and creative visualization will change a person's life. Jody must have faith in herself and her inner source to know she is never alone.

RELOCATION SPREAD

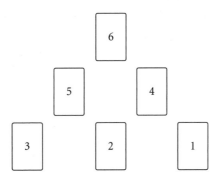

1. Why do I wish to relocate?
2. Is there a potential for a new job?
3. Is there a problem with my health in this area?
4. Will this move be successful financially?
5. Will I be happy in this new location?
6. Is it possible that this will be a permanent relocation?

Relocation Spread for Marty

Cards in the Spread

1st position	Ace of Swords
2nd position	Page of Pentacles
3rd position	King of Pentacles (reversed)
4th position	Ace of Wands
5th position	Queen of Wands (reversed)
6th position	Two of Pentacles (reversed)

Reading

Question 1: Why do I wish to relocate?

Answer: Ace of Swords. Marty ended a relationship and had a loss in his family, which made him very unhappy. Aces always indicate new beginnings and Marty could see new problems arising for him.

Question 2: Is there a potential for a new job?

Answer: Page of Pentacles. The potential for a new job is great, as is further schooling to go along with the job. It could mean on-the-job training, which Marty should accept.

Question 3: Is there a problem with my health in this area?

Answer: King of Pentacles (reversed). There could be health problems for Marty if he becomes lazy, too focused on sensual pleasures, or impractical with money. Marty is a Virgo, and work and health issues are Virgo's main drives. Earth signs are material and practical when positive, but greedy and grasping when negative. Balance is the answer.

Question 4: Will this move be successful financially?

Answer: Ace of Wands. Marty will have new beginnings in his work and social life. There will be opportunities for him in this move, both financially and socially. Marty should look forward to an exciting time during this period.

Question 5: Will I be happy in this new location?

Answer: Queen of Wands (reversed). This card can indicate a domineering, demanding, and controlling boss. Marty will need to do good work, be punctual, and be efficient to please this person. If Marty pays attention to his job, he can be happy.

Question 6: Is it possible that this will be a permanent relocation?

Answer: Two of Pentacles (reversed). Marty must learn as much as possible about his work, take care of his finances, and stay healthy. This card can indicate a lack of balance in money matters that Marty must overcome. Otherwise, the move might not work out.

Comments

This move could prove beneficial for Marty. It would change his environment and job and give him more potential options for new relationships. Now is the time to risk the move and make a new start.

PLANNING A VACATION

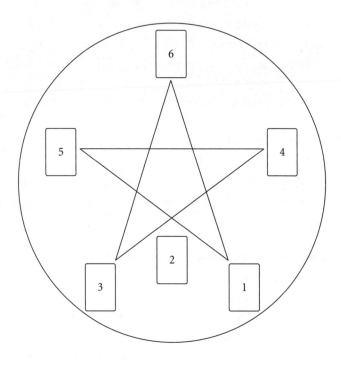

1. What kind of vacation do I prefer?
2. Shall I go alone?
3. Shall I go with others?
4. Will I enjoy myself and meet someone new?
5. Will there be any financial problems? Physical problems?
6. Do I need a vacation at this time?

Seven
Seeking Self-Knowledge

This chapter contains spreads that give information about oneself. The spreads are:

All About Me

What Is My Destiny?

Facing My Fears

Old Habit Patterns

Information Spread for the Past-Present-Future

The first four spreads have case studies that give you an idea about how to apply the tarot cards to the spread. The last one, Information Spread for the Past-Present-Future, does not have a case study, giving you the opportunity to exercise your intuition.

All five spreads are focused on the individual and his or her experiences. Each digs deeply into the psyche and helps heal the person's negative feelings. If anyone is seeking help to change his or her life, these are the spreads that are the best for that purpose. In doing the readings, the one most often chosen was All About Me.

ALL ABOUT ME

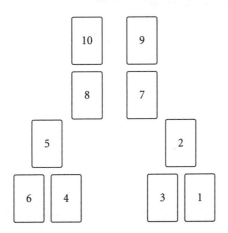

1. How do I get my ego needs fulfilled?
2. What influence does my mother still have on me?
3. What influence does my father still have on me?
4. Am I too self-critical?
5. What is my attitude toward sex and my body?
6. Are my choices regarding relationships good for me?
7. Do I have enough faith in myself to succeed?
8. What is my attitude toward my financial affairs?
9. In what ways do I feel victimized?
10. In what way can I change my life?

All About Me for Kerry

Cards in the Spread

1st position   Eight of Pentacles
2nd position   Nine of Swords (reversed)
3rd position   The Empress
4th position   Ten of Swords (reversed)
5th position   Ten of Cups
6th position   Temperance (reversed)
7th position   Three of Cups
8th position   Two of Cups
9th position   Judgement (reversed)
10th position   Five of Swords

Reading

Question 1: How do I get my ego needs fulfilled?

Answer: Eight of Pentacles. Kerry, a teacher, is learning about politics and ego needs. She ran for the office of coordinator at her school, but lost by a narrow margin. Kerry felt like an apprentice at that time but is more knowledgeable now. Her ego needs are most fulfilled by her work.

Question 2: What influence does my mother still have on me?

Answer: Nine of Swords (reversed). Kerry lacked wisdom regarding her problems but would not discuss them with her mother. There are ten children in Kerry's family and she wants her mom to love and accept her, even though she is a rebel. Kerry would like her mother to be more supportive and demonstrative.

Question 3: What influence does my father still have on me?

Answer: The Empress. Kerry's father is kind and gentle, and although she loves him, she may not respect him. When Dad is kind and gentle and Mom (the Empress) rules the roost, a child may feel confused about who is the boss in the home. If Kerry needed protection as a youngster and her dad failed to be there, she would feel vulnerable to males as an adult. Her problems with men stem from this early conditioning.

Question 4: Am I too self-critical?

Answer: Ten of Swords (reversed). Kerry is still carrying burdens from the past and judges herself too harshly. She wants change, but the only way that can happen is if she changes her thinking.

Question 5: What is my attitude toward sex and my body?

Answer: Ten of Cups. Kerry's attitude has changed for the better since she has been working with the tarot, and she has reached a higher emotional plane. The rainbow in the card is a sign of good luck and better things ahead.

Question 6: Are my choices regarding relationships good for me?

Answer: Temperance (reversed). Kerry's choices in relationships are not positive. There tends to be a lack of balance between her and her partner, causing emotional drain and much unhappiness. She must realize that she manifests her relationships based on old, negative patterns. She should meditate on her needs and desires before she gets involved with a new partner.

Question 7: Do I have enough faith in myself to succeed?

Answer: Three of Cups. Although Kerry's love relationships are not positive at this time, this card confirms that she has the skills to succeed, as evidenced by her career. By making positive, conscious choices, her personal life could be much more satisfying.

Question 8: What is my attitude toward my financial affairs?

Answer: Two of Cups. Kerry admitted that her finances are in sad shape; during the summer she plans to do extra work rather than spending her limited resources. She would like to have a relationship with a partner who could help her financially, but she realizes that is not a good reason for getting involved with someone.

Question 9: In what ways do I feel victimized?

Answer: Judgement (reversed). Kerry does not understand her own nature but is studying the tarot now, which will give her insight into herself. She is beginning to realize what part she is playing in her own life and that she is victimizing herself by remaining stuck in the past.

Question 10: In what way can I change my life?

Answer: Five of Swords. Kerry believes that relationships are too much trouble. She must learn that she does not need to fight with others to get her needs met. She needs to learn to love and trust herself.

Comments

Kerry's issues relate to her upbringing and family of origin. If she can learn to release the past, she can be much more happy and successful in the present.

All About Me for Gail

Cards in the Spread

1st position	Three of Wands (reversed)
2nd position	The Devil
3rd position	Six of Cups
4th position	Ace of Pentacles (reversed)
5th position	The Lovers (reversed)
6th position	Four of Cups
7th position	Seven of Swords (reversed)
8th position	Six of Pentacles (reversed)
9th position	The Hermit
10th position	Six of Swords (reversed)

Reading

Question 1: How do I get my ego needs fulfilled?

Answer: Three of Wands (reversed). Gail must ask herself what her ego needs are in order to fulfill them. She feels repressed— she does not make herself happy, go on trips, or communicate her desires.

Question 2: What influence does my mother still have on me?

Answer: The Devil. Gail feels oppressed by her mother, who is overly focused on materialism. Gail is caught up in this influence, but she can release herself by recognizing that she wants her mother to respond to her emotionally rather than by spending money on her.

Question 3: What influence does my father still have on me?

Answer: Six of Cups. Gail's parents were divorced when she was a little girl. She is still waiting for love from her father, which stands in the way of her relationships now. Gail must make a choice—whether to hold onto past hurts and feelings of rejection or to forgive her dad.

Question 4: Am I too self-critical?

Answer: Ace of Pentacles (reversed). Gail is judging herself too harshly and denying herself many life experiences. She just got a new job and makes more money, but still feels unworthy and insecure about her finances.

Question 5: What is my attitude toward sex and my body?

Answer: The Lovers (reversed). Gail has subconsciously rejected her sexual needs. She may be refusing to seek a new partner because her last relationship is not over emotionally. Gail claims she and her boyfriend are now "just friends," but the romance must be released completely so she can move on.

Question 6: Are my choices regarding relationships good for me?

Answer: Four of Cups. Gail is reflecting on her past relationships and not paying attention to what is being offered her in the present. If past partners have not been positive, then she is not making good choices. Gail must realize that she is out of balance and afraid to trust her heart for fear of being hurt. However, by changing the way she thinks, she can change the nature of her relationships.

Question 7: Do I have enough faith in myself to succeed?

Answer: Seven of Swords (reversed). Gail lacks faith in herself and focuses too much on the physical and material. She often feels cheated. Gail also feels that other people are creating her problems, rather than taking responsibility for her own actions.

Question 8: What is my attitude toward my financial affairs?

Answer: Six of Pentacles (reversed). Gail feels she has no choice in financial matters and believes others are in control of her money. In fact, Gail may not want to share her resources and feels guilty. Sharing is natural, but a child forced to share may grow up resentful and refuse to be charitable.

Question 9: In what ways do I feel victimized?

Answer: The Hermit. Gail feels unloved and alone, and is searching for a teacher or an inner guide. The Hermit is a Virgo card and her father is a Virgo who is very critical and judgmental. Gail rarely sees him and she would like to have a better relationship with him.

Question 10: In what way can I change my life?

Answer: Six of Swords (reversed). Gail thinks she does not have a choice in changing her life, but she does. She can change her life by changing her beliefs. Meditation and visualization are both methods that work.

Comments

All the sixes in this reading indicate that Gail can have a more positive, enjoyable life—if she so chooses. She can choose to blame her parents and others for her problems, or she can take responsibility, release the past, and move on to better things.

All About Me for Ruth

Cards in the Spread

1st position	Ten of Swords
2nd position	Three of Swords (reversed)
3rd position	Justice
4th position	Knight of Pentacles (reversed)
5th position	Six of Cups
6th position	Ace of Wands (reversed)
7th position	Four of Cups (reversed)
8th position	Seven of Wands
9th position	The Emperor (reversed)
10th position	The Devil (reversed)

Reading

Question 1: How do I get my ego needs fulfilled?

Answer: Ten of Swords. Ruth feels frustrated and unable to move forward, but soon some of her burdens will be lifted. If she is waiting for someone else to fulfill her ego needs, she will not be satisfied; she must fulfill her own ego needs, not wait for others to do it.

Question 2: What influence does my mother still have on me?

Answer: Three of Swords (reversed). Ruth has always had problems with her mother and has never felt accepted by her. Now Ruth and her two daughters are living with her mom, and Ruth and a friend are planning to go on a cruise. She feels guilty and selfish about spending money on the trip. Also, some of her friends have recently proved untrustworthy and she is insecure and confused.

Question 3: What influence does my father still have on me?

Answer: Justice. As a child, Ruth loved her father but felt rejected by him, which set up a pattern for her in relationships with other men. She is divorced and was upset to learn that her two daughters also felt abandoned by their father. Old habit patterns are difficult to break, especially when people refuse to notice they keep repeating the same kind of experiences. Ruth agreed with this analysis.

Question 4: Am I too self-critical?

Answer: Knight of Pentacles (reversed). This Knight does not bring good news about money or indicates that messages were not received. Ruth may be subconsciously denying herself a loving relationship, a home of her own, or money due to her early experiences with her parents.

Question 5: What is my attitude toward sex and my body?

Answer: Six of Cups. Ruth is living in the past. Her past experiences were not very positive, and neither are her memories. She is overweight, which is not good for her body or her self-esteem. If Ruth won't take care of her own needs, who will? She must make better choices.

Question 6: Are my choices regarding relationships good for me?

Answer: Ace of Wands (reversed). This card indicates a lack of activity where work or social life are concerned. Ruth does not respect men, so any relationship she attracts would be problematic. With understanding, she could change her attitude and change her life.

Question 7: Do I have enough faith in myself to succeed?

Answer: Four of Cups (reversed). Ruth does not realize she is keeping herself from success. She doesn't feel loved, fears a commitment, and has been disappointed in her relationships. She has unrealistic expectations, which stop her from getting involved. Faith to succeed comes from loving oneself and being willing to work toward one's goals.

Question 8: What is my attitude toward my financial affairs?

Answer: Seven of Wands. Ruth has the ability to be successful in business or socially, if she wants to be. She is a Cancer who needs to feel nurtured, safe, and secure. Having a home of her own is important to her, yet she is living with her mother and working part-time.

Question 9: In what ways do I feel victimized?

Answer: The Emperor (reversed). Ruth does not realize her potential. With the right attitude, she could be a leader or work in a management position. Presently, however, she is fearful, immature, lacking balance, and not always honest with herself and others. Ruth is not as warm and loving as she thinks and likes to control her environment. She is a good actress and believes the part she is playing. Ruth victimizes herself without realizing what she is doing because she lacks self-awareness. It is time for her to wake up and make changes.

Question 10: In what way can I change my life?

Answer: The Devil (reversed). Ruth must take a hard, realistic look at her life and her choices. She could take more responsibility for her life and be a positive example for her daughters. Losing weight should be a priority and would improve her self-esteem.

Comments

What a person believes will manifest in his or her life. Consciousness is all we have to work with, and by paying attention to our thinking, we realize why our lives are the way they are. Ruth was able to see, through the tarot cards, how she could change her life in ways she never would have considered.

WHAT IS MY DESTINY?

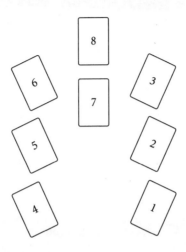

1. Will my life change soon?
2. Is there a new relationship ahead for me?
3. What chance is there for my ex-lover's return?
4. What is my potential to win or inherit money?
5. Is there a trip in my future?
6. Am I working out my karma?
7. Will I have a long and happy life?
8. Will I marry more than one time?

What Is My Destiny for Eric

Cards in the Spread

1st position	Page of Pentacles
2nd position	Seven of Swords (reversed)
3rd position	The Devil (reversed)
4th position	The Star (reversed)
5th position	The Moon (reversed)
6th position	The Hanged Man (reversed)
7th position	King of Cups
8th position	Four of Wands

Reading

Question 1: Will my life change soon?

Answer: Page of Pentacles. This Page indicates a scholar, someone who wants to earn money to go to college and get a good education. Eric is almost fifteen and is determined to have a career in math or science. He and his family were on vacation in northern California at the time of this reading, so there were already changes underway in his life.

Question 2: Is there a new relationship ahead for me?

Answer: Seven of Swords (reversed). Eric does not have a relationship at this time. He did not like leaving his friends and almost refused to go with his family on this trip. However, Eric is quite involved with his schoolwork and a little immature to have a boy-girl relationship.

Question 3: What chance is there for my ex-lover's return?

Answer: The Devil (reversed). There is no ex or present lover for Eric. There is, however, a decrease in selfishness or greed for material possessions. He is beginning to accept responsibility and face the reality of life. A change of diet would improve his health.

Question 4: What is my potential to win or inherit money?

Answer: The Star (reversed). Eric is not optimistic about his career, his life in general, or his goals. He must change his attitude now in order to have a more productive life. He is a Virgo, and people of this sign always feel they must "work" for anything they want. Winning would be against their belief system.

Question 5: Is there a trip in my future?

Answer: The Moon (reversed). Eric is on that trip now. His mother is a teacher and plans family trips around educational destinations. This does not always please the rest of the family and they feel forced to go. Eric feels emotionally stressed by the vacation.

Question 6: Am I working out my karma?

Answer: The Hanged Man (reversed). This card symbolizes a person who is not aware of or who does not trust his or her inner source. Eric is stubborn, focused on the material world, and does not accept new information easily—

traits not uncommon among teenagers. With maturity, he will become more aware of karmic patterns in his life.

Question 7: Will I have a long and happy life?

Answer: King of Cups. This King represents an older man, so this would indicate a long life. As Eric grows up, he will become more loving and aware. If Eric feels safe and secure in his professional life and within himself, he will have a good and joyous life.

Question 8: Will I marry more than one time?

Answer: Four of Wands. Eric believes that when he gets married it will be permanent, balanced, and fruitful. He wants a solid partnership with a good social life. It's up to him—and his choice of partner—whether he will marry more than once.

Comments

Eric was apprehensive when I asked him to do this spread; all the reversed cards indicate his unwillingness to participate. He must realize that, even at age fourteen or fifteen, one's thoughts and beliefs create one's reality.

What Is My Destiny for Valery

Cards in the Spread

1st position	The World
2nd position	Seven of Swords (reversed)
3rd position	Page of Swords (reversed)
4th position	The Wheel of Fortune
5th position	Four of Swords (reversed)
6th position	Five of Wands
7th position	Queen of Pentacles
8th position	King of Cups

Reading

Question 1: Will my life change soon?

Answer: The World. This card symbolizes success in all endeavors and the attainment of all goals. Valery must have faith that all is well; she is being supported by her inner source and victory is assured. There will be new opportunities, trips, a new job, or a residential move.

Question 2: Is there a new relationship ahead for me?

Answer: Seven of Swords (reversed). If there is a new relationship, it will not last long. Valery creates her own problems, though they are temporary. She may feel cheated or have trouble trusting others. Valery must be prepared for new experiences by being open and honest.

Question 3: What chance is there for my ex-lover's return?

Answer: Page of Swords (reversed). This Page has many troubles and is not a free thinker. Valery must examine her motives if she wants this type of person to come back into her life.

Question 4: What is my potential to win or inherit money?

Answer: The Wheel of Fortune. This card indicates that it is time for Valery to take a chance, gamble, or travel. Success in money matters—even a windfall of some kind—is likely at this time. Now is the time to let go of old ties that are a burden in business or relationships.

Question 5: Is there a trip in my future?

Answer: Four of Swords (reversed). A trip for Valery at this time would be beneficial, and a period of rest could aid her health. She has been stretching the limits of her physical body and creating inner tension. She needs a change in her environment and a trip is the best answer.

Question 6: Am I working out my karma?

Answer: Five of Wands. Valery wants to promote her own ideas at work and in her social life, but her ego needs cause dissension and must be curbed. She has family strife and many challenges with her coworkers. To work out her karma, Valery could try to be more loving and understanding of others.

Question 7: Will I have a long and happy life?

Answer: Queen of Pentacles. This Queen is an earth sign, as is Valery; as a rule, these people have strong and healthy bodies. However, there is a tendency toward being overly critical, an idealist, and a perfectionist. Valery should have a long life—however, happiness will be a choice.

Question 8: Will I marry more than one time?

Answer: King of Cups. This King is emotional, loving, caring, and nurturing. When married, he is a good family man. As long as he feels secure in a situation, he will remain. Valery would do well to marry this type of man. If she does, a lasting marriage is likely. If not, more than one marriage is probable.

Comments

Valery's future looks bright and shows a lot of potential. Although she still has some emotional blocks, particularly where relationships are concerned, overall the reading was positive. Valery should feel good about her future.

FACING MY FEARS

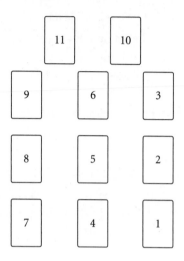

1. What am I afraid of?
2. Is my safety or security at risk?
3. Is there someone to whom I can communicate my fears to get help?
4. Are my fears focused at my workplace?
5. Do my fears concern sex or injury to my person?
6. Are these fears creating health problems for me?
7. Do my fears involve other people?
8. Do my fears stem from a lack of self-confidence or feelings of inadequacy?
9. Why do I feel like a victim?
10. What type of changes can I make to overcome my fears?
11. Final outcome?

Facing My Fears for Olivia

Cards in the Spread

1st position	Ten of Pentacles (reversed)
2nd position	Page of Pentacles (reversed)
3rd position	The Empress (reversed)
4th position	The Fool
5th position	Four of Cups
6th position	Nine of Cups (reversed)
7th position	Ace of Wands
8th position	Knight of Wands (reversed)
9th position	Seven of Wands
10th position	Nine of Swords (reversed)
11th position	Ten of Cups (reversed)

Reading

Question 1: What am I afraid of?

Answer: Ten of Pentacles (reversed). Olivia fears not having money and does not feel that her finances can ever change for the better. Olivia is not prosperity-minded, an attitude that stems from her early childhood.

Question 2: Is my safety or security at risk?

Answer: Page of Pentacles (reversed). Olivia did not continue her education past high school and does not have a professional career. She feels that her earning power is limited and getting a good-paying job is not possible. Olivia's security needs are in jeopardy and by going back to school, her earning potential can be increased. This will make her feel safer and more secure in the future.

Question 3: Is there someone to whom I can communicate my fears to get help?

Answer: The Empress (reversed). Olivia does not feel her mother will be of any assistance to her and has no love relationship at this time, which leaves her feeling alone and vulnerable. She needs a counselor and could find one at school if she decides to go.

Question 4: Are my fears focused at my workplace?

Answer: The Fool. Olivia is bored with her job. She wants new experiences, activity, and adventure in her life. She must use caution and pay attention to her surroundings, as well as being more aware of her attitude, which has been careless about finances in the past.

Question 5: Do my fears concern sex or injury to my person?

Answer: Four of Cups. Olivia is hanging on to past experiences that were not positive. She may have been hurt emotionally and fears getting involved with the same type of experience. Olivia must change her mental attitude and trust her instincts.

Question 6: Are these fears creating health problems for me?

Answer: Nine of Cups (reversed). This card indicates an emotional drain and unhappiness in love. Olivia suffered a loss in her most recent relationship and, by dwelling on this negativity, her health is affected. She did not want to end the affair, even though it was not positive. Olivia must learn to control her emotions and have a healthier outlook on life.

Question 7: Do my fears involve other people?

Answer: Ace of Wands. Olivia will be making new business and social contacts and will have new beginnings and opportunities. If she fears these contacts, she will miss out on the opportunities.

Question 8: Do my fears stem from a lack of self-confidence or feelings of inadequacy?

Answer: Knight of Wands (reversed). Olivia hates delays and frequently becomes frustrated both on the job and with her lack of social outings. She has not been very active socially, which makes her feel less self-confident.

Question 9: Why do I feel like a victim?

Answer: Seven of Wands. Because Olivia does not have a good job or a love relationship at this time, she may feel others do not respect her. She must focus on her goals and take charge of her life. Feeling like a victim is demeaning and Olivia must always respect herself.

Question 10: What type of changes can I make to overcome my fears?

Answer: Nine of Swords (reversed). Olivia is in a state of crisis that may soon come to a head. She must learn to trust her inner self and seek guidance from within. By recognizing her problems, answers will soon come to her—

becoming aware is the first step toward a solution. Taking positive action is the next step.

Question 11: Final outcome?

Answer: Ten of Cups (reversed). Olivia's family makes her feel emotionally drained and she does not expect to see immediate changes in her relationships with family members. They are not supportive of her desire to go back to school or find a better job. Olivia wants to change others, which is impossible. She can only change herself.

Comments

Olivia is going through a rough period in her life, but it will strengthen her resolve to make her life better. She must learn to avoid relationships that drain her emotionally. The time is right to return to school or broaden her horizons.

OLD HABIT PATTERNS

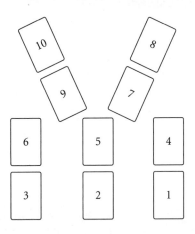

1. What are my negative habit patterns?
2. How are they affecting my life?
3. How can I become aware of these patterns?
4. Are other people involved with my past patterns?
5. Will I be able to overcome these patterns?
6. What decisions must I make now?
7. Should I seek professional help?
8. Do I have the confidence to confront these old patterns?
9. What changes can I expect when I rid myself of these old habit patterns?
10. Final outcome?

Old Habit Patterns for Ellie

Cards in the Spread

1st position	King of Wands
2nd position	The Tower
3rd position	Six of Pentacles (reversed)
4th position	Nine of Pentacles
5th position	Four of Wands (reversed)
6th position	The Moon
7th position	Four of Pentacles
8th position	The Hierophant (reversed)
9th position	Queen of Cups
10th position	The Wheel of Fortune (reversed)

Reading

Question 1: What are my negative habit patterns?

Answer: King of Wands. Ellie has a good friend who helps her with business transactions and she has some fears about trusting her own judgment. This friend likes to start things but doesn't always stay to finish up, which Ellie enjoys doing. It should make her feel accomplished when she finishes any business deal in a positive manner.

Question 2: How are they affecting my life?

Answer: The Tower. This card indicates Ellie must throw out her old habits and learn to depend on herself. This friend may decide to leave unexpectedly and Ellie must be prepared to make her own decisions. She may have sudden insights into future events—if she is aware of this possibility, she will not feel abandoned.

Question 3: How can I become aware of these patterns?

Answer: Six of Pentacles (reversed). This card indicates that Ellie does not make decisions regarding her finances. This is not wise of her and she must change her attitude about money immediately. Ellie must take control of her life and not lean on others. Meditation and seeking truth can make it easier for her to institute changes now.

Question 4: Are other people involved with my past patterns?

Answer: Nine of Pentacles. Ellie is in business and it is natural to assume that she has been involved with others. She enjoys being an independent woman of means and people are attracted to her because she is a winner. Although she has money, she seems to lack ideas that would increase her business, so she constantly seeks help from those who have creative skills.

Question 5: Will I be able to overcome these patterns?

Answer: Four of Wands (reversed). Ellie feels uncertain at this time. She fears her business may decline, that she will have financial problems, and that she will have no one to rely on. This is negative thinking, which can attract exactly those experiences she fears. Ellie can overcome these patterns by thinking positively, sending love to all, and having faith in herself.

Question 6: What decisions must I make now?

Answer: The Moon. Ellie must face the truth in all of her experiences and learn to control her negative thinking, fears, and doubts. Ellie would be wise to use her intuition more in her business dealings, especially where people are concerned.

Question 7: Should I seek professional help?

Answer: Four of Pentacles. Ellie needs a more balanced, realistic attitude regarding money. Seeking the services of a financial advisor or trustworthy accountant would be a worthwhile investment.

Question 8: Do I have the confidence to confront these old patterns?

Answer: The Hierophant (reversed). At this time, Ellie may not think she has the confidence, but this can change. She needs new information to help her grow and become a confident woman with faith in herself. Ellie has untapped inner resources and perhaps now is the time for her to become aware of her potential.

Question 9: What changes can I expect when I rid myself of these old habit patterns?

Answer: Queen of Cups. This Queen is powerful, intuitive, and intense. She desires control in her environment. Ellie can expect to acquire these traits within herself. She can be in control of her life and make her own decisions with confidence.

Question 10: Final outcome?

Answer: The Wheel of Fortune (reversed). Ellie should not gamble or take risks at this time. No new ventures or serious relationships should be started now. She needs to focus her energies on putting her finances in order and strengthening her self-esteem.

Comments

Ellie would be wise to seek professional help to become more self-sufficient and in control of her life. She needs friends so she can enjoy herself away from work.

INFORMATION SPREAD FOR THE PAST–PRESENT–FUTURE

Future	4	3	2	1
Present	4	3	2	1
Past	4	3	2	1

The Past: These cards can refer to yesterday or several years ago, but the information still has an influence on the querent's life.

The Present: These cards refer to the querent's thoughts and beliefs now.

The Future: These cards represent the querent's subconscious mind. Events may happen immediately or within the next few months.

To Begin This Spread

Shuffle the cards and hand them to the querent. The querent should shuffle the cards and hand them back to you. They can cut the cards once, twice, or three times, whichever they prefer.

Place the first card face up in the first position, beginning with the "Past" row, and then continue until all twelve cards have been laid out. Before you begin the reading, examine the spread. See which of the four elements appear in the spread and check for repeated numbers (how many ones, twos, or threes, etc.). Also, look at how many major arcana cards and court cards are present. These indicate people involved with the querent. If there are many of these cards, this may indicate that there are too many people involved in the affairs of the querent. All of this information is helpful to you, the reader.

To Read This Spread

When you speak of the past, remember to use past tense and phrases such as "in the past" or "previously." For cards relating to the present, your sentences should begin with "now" or "presently." For cards relating to the future, you could begin with "in the future," "soon," and so on.

This spread will show you how the person is thinking and, through the spread, you will have the opportunity to provide him or her with new information that may change his or her thoughts or beliefs. This is a serious responsibility for the reader because, as we have seen, one's thoughts have the power to change one's life. The reader must have integrity and confidence. Remember always to be truthful, while ending the reading on a positive note whenever possible.

Eight

Spiritual Seekers

All four spreads in this chapter relate to work being done by the individual to understand some aspect of his or her life's purpose. Each has sample readings.

The spreads are:

Spiritual Aspiration

Reincarnation

Contacting Spirit Guides

Soul Mate

Relax and give yourself plenty of time to work with the fifteen questions included in the Reincarnation spread. The Soul Mate spread has eleven questions, while Spiritual Aspiration has only seven. The Contacting Spirit Guides has nine.

These spreads are fun to do and you will receive some valuable information at the same time. Be sure to involve the querent in conversation during the readings, and don't forget to try them out for yourself.

SPIRITUAL ASPIRATION

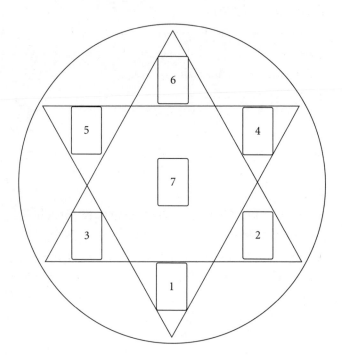

1. What is my attitude toward physical and material concerns?
2. How do I maintain my emotional balance?
3. Will I find a teacher soon?
4. What are the blocks to my enlightenment?
5. What changes must I make now?
6. What are my choices now?
7. What is my connection to my inner self and a Higher Source?

Spiritual Aspiration for Jenny

Cards in the Spread

1st position	The Emperor
2nd position	Ten of Wands
3rd position	The High Priestess
4th position	Eight of Swords (reversed)
5th position	Seven of Pentacles
6th position	The Hermit (reversed)
7th position	Six of Wands

Reading

Question 1: What is my attitude toward physical and material concerns?

Answer: The Emperor. Jenny realizes she is the boss, leader, and initiator of her actions. She is independent and has good ideas. Jenny is in touch with her inner source, which helps her to keep her physical and material desires in perspective.

Question 2: How do I maintain my emotional balance?

Answer: Ten of Wands. Jenny keeps her emotions in balance by refusing to accept the burdens of others. There are constant changes in Jenny's workplace and new people to deal with every day, and she could have a lot of stress if she did not maintain adequate boundaries.

Question 3: Will I find a teacher soon?

Answer: The High Priestess. This card infers that Jenny understands a great deal on an intuitive level. She must listen to her inner source for guidance and then apply the knowledge. She will find her teacher within herself.

Question 4: What are the blocks to my enlightenment?

Answer: Eight of Swords (reversed). Jenny does not feel she has the strength to overcome her problems and feels "stuck." It is only a belief, however, and it can be changed at any time through meditation. The underlying issue could be fear of enlightenment and the ensuing responsibilities.

Question 5: What changes must I make now?

Answer: Seven of Pentacles. Jenny is in a position to harvest the fruits of her labors, but she must not let her ego get in the way of her desire to be of service to others. Rather than "coasting" at work, she must continue to persevere.

Question 6: What are my choices now?

Answer: The Hermit (reversed). Jenny has choices to make, but they must be made with confidence and an open mind. There could be fear or some insecurity that must be dealt with first. She may not be in touch with her inner teacher at this time and should make an effort to meditate.

Question 7: What is my connection to my inner self and a Higher Source?

Answer: Six of Wands. This is the card of victory! Jenny can be victorious by continuing to develop her connection to her inner teacher, which will help her to make positive choices at work and socially. She must balance her desires and ego needs with faith in herself and her inner resources.

Comments

Jenny would like to start a center to teach spiritual values, meditation, and related subjects. She has the power to make it happen!

Spiritual Aspiration for Lilly

Cards in the Spread

1st position	Two of Pentacles (reversed)
2nd position	Knight of Swords
3rd position	The Wheel of Fortune
4th position	Ace of Wands
5th position	Nine of Swords (reversed)
6th position	Two of Swords (reversed)
7th position	Four of Wands

Reading

Question 1: What is my attitude toward physical and material concerns?

Answer: Two of Pentacles (reversed). Lilly feels she does not know how to handle money. She does not like to budget and she is materialistically focused. She likes to spend money on others as well as herself, however, so she is not greedy or stingy.

Question 2: How do I maintain my emotional balance?

Answer: Knight of Swords. Lilly is a Leo and a very strong individual. Because she likes to help others, she attracts people who have problems and then becomes embroiled in those problems herself. However, she has her own issues that she must attend to first. Lilly tends to let her emotions overrule her reason; her challenge is to balance her heart and her head.

Question 3: Will I find a teacher soon?

Answer: The Wheel of Fortune. Now is the time for Lilly to make changes, take a trip, or gamble. Let go of old ties— business or personal—that are a burden and seek happiness during this peak period. Lilly should realize that life is experience and everything she does or has done makes her who she is today. Life has been her teacher up to this point; with the changes she makes, she may find a teacher she could accept.

Question 4: What are the blocks to my enlightenment?

Answer: Ace of Wands. Lilly desires new beginnings in her work and social life. She wants excitement, pleasure, and relationships. However, enlightenment comes through meditation, doing good works, and the inward search for one's source. When Lilly ends her focus on just the "outer" world, she will begin to find enlightenment.

Question 5: What changes must I make now?

Answer: Nine of Swords (reversed). The changes Lilly must make include facing her problems, trusting her intuition, and evaluating her experiences to gain wisdom. She must have faith in herself and release her grandiose expectations that lead to disappointments. Leo is the sign of the ego, which must be controlled in spiritual work. Learning to meditate is highly recommended for Lilly.

Question 6: What are my choices now?

Answer: Two of Swords (reversed). Since Lilly does not want to see her problems and issues, she will continue to struggle with them. She has a fear of seeing herself realistically due to her ego needs. Her illusory thinking about life and the world in which she lives gives her a materialistic focus, and she must choose between this and gaining a more spiritual outlook.

Question 7: What is my connection to my inner self and a Higher Source?

Answer: Four of Wands. Lilly's work and social activities are fulfilling and enjoyable, but she does not have as much faith in herself in relationships as she does in her work abilities. Lilly is just beginning to get in touch with her inner self and to consider the existence of a Higher Source. At this time, she has other priorities beyond the pursuit of spiritual aspirations—what she really wants right now is to buy a condominium!

Comments

Lilly is a flight attendant and enjoys her work. She likes the excitement of going to foreign countries and meeting people. She is divorced but wants to get married again someday. She is not motivated to turn her full attention to spiritual work at present.

REINCARNATION SPREAD

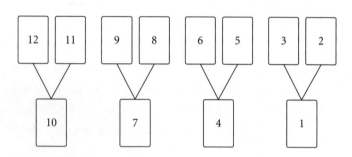

1. Who was I in my most recent lifetime?
2. Was I married?
3. Was I happy in this past life?
4. What kind of work did I do in that life?
5. Was I an honorable person?
6. What type of problems and challenges did I deal with?
7. Was I a famous person?
8. Was my health good during my past life?
9. How did I die?
10. Did I have a soul mate?
11. Is my present love relationship someone I knew during my past life?
12. Am I linked to my parents of today from my past life?

13. Are any other members of my family from my past life?
14. What do I need to learn during this lifetime?
15. Will I reincarnate after this life?

Reincarnation Spread for Daniel

Cards in the Spread

1st position	Seven of Swords (reversed)
2nd position	Five of Wands (reversed)
3rd position	The Hermit (reversed)
4th position	Two of Cups
5th position	The Fool
6th position	Strength
7th position	The Empress
8th position	Four of Pentacles (reversed)
9th position	Page of Swords
10th position	Two of Pentacles
11th position	Eight of Wands (reversed)
12th position	Six of Wands
13th position	Nine of Pentacles (reversed)
14th position	Nine of Cups
15th position	Nine of Wands (reversed)

Reading

Question 1: Who was I in my most recent lifetime?

Answer: Seven of Swords (reversed). Daniel was not happy in his last life. He was jealous, materially focused, and in relationships that were not positive. According to the cards in his spread, he had problems with work and money situations. Also, Daniel may have been a woman, indicated by the presence of the Empress in the seventh position of this spread. (This is not unusual, as we all incarnate as both male and female over the course of many lifetimes.)

Question 2: Was I married?

Answer: Five of Wands (reversed). This card indicates that Daniel was married, although he and his partner did not have a good relationship. Daniel needed more faith and confidence in himself and he may not have fought for his rights.

Question 3: Was I happy in this past life?

Answer: The Hermit (reversed). Daniel lacked wisdom or insight, and was selfish and intolerant. He was focused on physical and material possessions. If he'd been happy, he would not have been greedy in his need for these things.

Question 4: What kind of work did I do in that life?

Answer: Two of Cups. This card may indicate that Daniel sought marriage as a means to fulfill his potential. If he was a female, that would have been the natural thing to do; being a wife, mother, and nurturer was a woman's role in most past cultures.

Question 5: Was I an honorable person?

Answer: The Fool. This card would show that Daniel, in that lifetime, was interested in new experiences, activity, and adventure, and did not use his intelligence wisely. He

may have been honorable, but others may have judged
him harshly.

Question 6: What type of problems and challenges did I deal with?

Answer. Strength. Daniel had problems with leadership,
controlling his passions, and resisting temptation. All of
these things were challenges to his role in life. Daniel was
also artistic and creative during that lifetime.

Question 7: Was I a famous person?

Answer: The Empress. This card would suggest that Daniel
was indeed a famous person, perhaps a female in a position of power.

Question 8: Was my health good during my past life?

Answer: Four of Pentacles (reversed). There may have been
a lack of balance in Daniel's life or he may have been too
busy enjoying himself. Excessive spending or money problems would have affected his health adversely, as would
conflict in his marriage.

Question 9: How did I die?

Answer: Page of Swords. This card indicates that Daniel
might have died young, perhaps by the sword or guillo-
tine. He had many desires, and was naive, unconventional,
and extroverted. Daniel did not pay attention to his socie-
tal role and his circumstances, and that may have cost him
his life.

Question 10: Did I have a soul mate?

Answer: Two of Pentacles. The Two of Cups and Two of Pentacles in the spread indicate the presence of a soul mate, someone who tried to maintain a balance in money and health. If Daniel wanted material possessions, to live life to the fullest, or wanted new adventures constantly, the ability to juggle everything fell to the soul mate.

Question 11: Is my present love relationship someone I knew during my past life?

Answer: Eight of Wands (reversed). Daniel does not have a love relationship at this time. He has had several involvements during this lifetime, but none that lasted. Perhaps he fears repeating his negative experiences from past lifetimes—a common fear for most of us.

Question 12: Am I linked to my parents of today from my past life?

Answer: Six of Wands. This card refers to making choices, being responsible, and taking control of one's life. It states that Daniel made a choice about his parents in this lifetime. His parents provided him with an upbringing that ensures his success in his chosen work and in his social life.

Question 13: Are any other members of my family from my past life?

Answer: Nine of Pentacles (reversed). This card suggests that some family members were connected through finances. Daniel has had to learn to work and take care of his own financial burdens. He cannot depend entirely on family, relationships, or others for support.

Question 14: What do I need to learn during this lifetime?

Answer: Nine of Cups. Daniel must learn to love wisely and have self-confidence and self-esteem. This is the "wish card" and when it appears upright, it means you will get your wish. In this case, it means that Daniel will successfully learn his lessons concerning love and his emotional needs.

Question 15: Will I reincarnate after this life?

Answer: Nine of Wands (reversed). Daniel feels that he would rather not. He does not like competition in the business world or in society, for he is more passive and would prefer to handle his affairs in a more spiritual way. It's unlikely that he's reached the end of the cycle of reincarnation; however, with four of the number nine cards present in this spread, including the Hermit, he may be allowed to "take a break" from life on earth for a while.

Comments

The interpretation of this reading is all conjecture, but as humans we store information in our cells regarding our past, present, and future. There are many reversed cards in Daniel's spread. It seems that he does not have clear memories regarding his past life. Work, money, and emotional relationships were issues for Daniel and it seems the same ones are happening to him again. Until we learn our lessons, we are fated to repeat them.

Reincarnation Spread for Renee

Cards in the Spread

1st position	Six of Cups (reversed)
2nd position	Four of Cups (reversed)
3rd position	The Tower
4th position	Five of Cups (reversed)
5th position	The Empress
6th position	Death
7th position	Knight of Cups
8th position	Strength
9th position	King of Wands
10th position	Ten of Swords
11th position	Queen of Wands
12th position	Three of Wands
13th position	Six of Wands
14th position	The Wheel of Fortune (reversed)
15th position	Nine of Swords

Reading

Question 1: Who was I in my most recent lifetime?

Answer: Six of Cups (reversed). Renee was a person who may have refused to make decisions and stayed close to her family. She was emotionally drained and there was a potential for illness in her past life that may have severely afflicted her.

Question 2: Was I married?

Answer: Four of Cups (reversed). Renee may have been afraid of an emotional relationship. She feared being hurt by someone she loved, so she may not have married. There may have been a lack of emotional balance, a missing father figure, or some dishonesty.

Question 3: Was I happy in this past life?

Answer: The Tower. This card indicates that Renee received enlightenment and learned a great deal during this past life. She managed to get rid of some false ideas and old habit patterns. There was strife, but there were also some good times.

Question 4: What kind of work did I do in that life?

Answer: Five of Cups (reversed). This card declares that Renee did not believe in love. There may have been several losses in the family, relationships, or friends that hurt her. She felt she might have been a church leader. There may have been great disappointments for her during that time and the church offered some protection.

Question 5: Was I an honorable person?

Answer: The Empress. Yes. Renee was creative and nurturing, especially as a mature woman. She knew how to communicate with others, loved to help people, and enjoyed traveling.

Question 6: What type of problems and challenges did I deal with?

Answer: Death. There were lessons for Renee regarding death and dying. She may have gotten in the way of other people's karma by trying to save them. Transformation was a challenge for Renee and people were constantly going in and out of her life.

Question 7: Was I a famous person?

Answer: Knight of Cups. Renee was well-known, as she was forever receiving messages of all kinds. She was always getting invitations to attend functions from family, friends, and others in high standing. She wished to do service work and help others. Renee may have traveled and visited far-off places.

Question 8: Was my health good during my past life?

Answer: Strength. Yes. Although there were indications of an illness early in life, Renee was able to handle her problems and maintain a balance in that life. She had courage and fortitude, and used her power wisely.

Question 9: How did I die?

Answer: King of Wands. Renee felt that she died alone. This is an Aries card and could show some type of mental problems or a stroke. As Aries rules the head, she may have been shot in the head by a man. Whatever happened, it was a sudden death.

Question 10: Did I have a soul mate?

Answer: Ten of Swords. During that lifetime, Renee sought to raise her consciousness and experienced major inner transformation. She was very busy trying to lift her burdens and overcome negative experiences and so did not feel her soul mate made an appearance during that lifetime.

Question 11: Is my present love relationship someone I knew during my past life?

Answer: Queen of Wands. Renee said she had no love relationship at this time. As this is a Leo card, perhaps she needs to incorporate such Leo traits such as playfulness, generosity, and extroversion into her present life to attract a love relationship.

Question 12: Am I linked to my parents of today from my past life?

Answer: Three of Wands. Renee feels a strong link to her mother. She also feels she was involved with her father, but not as closely.

Question 13: Are any other members of my family from my past life?

Answer: Six of Wands. Renee has nine siblings and feels that some of them were involved in her past life. She thinks that some were very good workers and successful during that time.

Question 14: What do I need to learn during this lifetime?

Answer: The Wheel of Fortune (reversed). This card, reversed, signifies that Renee does not have major lessons to learn in this lifetime; rather, she should concentrate on internalizing past lessons. It is not the time to begin new ventures or take chances and she needs to be honest in all her experiences. Her lessons now relate to more stability and less risk-taking with her life and time.

Question 15: Will I reincarnate after this life?

Answer: Nine of Swords. This card indicates wisdom gained through experience with problems and troubles. The mention of reincarnating again put Renee in crisis as she felt this time was sufficient. She said, "Do this again? Never!"

Comments

The Empress card may indicate that Renee held a position of high regard in this past life, perhaps in a religious capacity. It seems she had some unfortunate experiences early on, but her life was devoted to service and she learned a great deal in that lifetime.

CONTACTING SPIRIT GUIDES

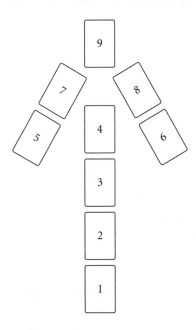

1. Do I have spirit guides?
2. How can I contact my spirit guides?
3. Will I make contact with my spirit guides soon?
4. Will we communicate only mentally?
5. Have my spirit guides been with me always?
6. Will my guides give me information about my work, home matters, and relationships?
7. Can my guides teach me about other realities?
8. Do spirit guides appear in physical form?
9. Final outcome?

Contacting Spirit Guides for Shirley

Cards in the Spread

1st position	Six of Wands
2nd position	Seven of Pentacles (reversed)
3rd position	The Hermit (reversed)
4th position	Two of Swords
5th position	King of Wands (reversed)
6th position	The Fool (reversed)
7th position	Ten of Wands (reversed)
8th position	The World
9th position	Knight of Swords (reversed)

Reading

Question 1: Do I have spirit guides?

Answer: Six of Wands. The answer is yes for everyone who believes in spirit guides. This card symbolizes making decisions and being successful. Shirley is using her will and energy in positive ways, mentally, physically, and emotionally. Her guides are with her, even though she may not realize it.

Question 2: How can I contact my spirit guides?

Answer: Seven of Pentacles (reversed). Shirley is being positive in many ways, but it is possible that she does not have much self-confidence. Through meditation and concentration Shirley could contact her guides—it is a good way to get started.

Question 3: Will I make contact with my spirit guides soon?

Answer: The Hermit (reversed). Shirley can be closed-minded and prejudiced. She must examine her fears concerning contacting her guides. Shirley must realize her guides are there to help, not to threaten her or try to control her.

Question 4: Will we communicate only mentally?

Answer: Two of Swords. Shirley says she knows about her spirit guides but she doesn't want to "see" them. She is not using her intuition, so things are not clear. If Shirley does not want to see her guides, when she does make contact, it can only be mentally.

Question 5: Have my spirit guides been with me always?

Answer: King of Wands (reversed). The possibility is that one's guides do not stay in one place; rather, they come and go based on one's needs at any given time. This card is an Aries, and Aries people like to be on the go. It may be that Shirley has guides who like to play and have fun (Aries types can be like children). This could be a message for Shirley to lighten up.

Question 6: Will my guides give me information about my work, home matters, and relationships?

Answer: The Fool (reversed). Shirley must take responsibility for balancing relationships, sexual needs, and the other desires in her life. Her guides will try to focus her attention on spiritual matters and let her make decisions about worldly issues.

Question 7: Can my guides teach me about other realities?

Answer: Ten of Wands (reversed). Shirley must realize that her guides can teach her many things. She is seeking relief from burdens in her work and social life but does not seem to be interested in spiritual information. Shirley feels this is a "fad" that will soon pass, but she is not right. Spirit is and will always be. Our guides are with us even if we fail to acknowledge them.

Question 8: Do spirit guides appear in physical form?

Answer: The World. There is nothing that spirit guides cannot do. Usually, the guides are seen in one's consciousness, but anything is possible. Shirley must have faith and trust.

Question 9: Final outcome?

Answer: Knight of Swords (reversed). Shirley may not get any messages at this time regarding her spirit guides, but she should keep trying if she is sincere.

Comments

There are many new students in spiritual work and Shirley is one of them. Many are in a hurry to attain the knowledge others have spent years gathering. The sooner Shirley can release her fears and maintain an open mind, the sooner she'll make contact with her guides.

Contacting Spirit Guides for Penny

Cards in the Spread

1st position	Five of Swords
2nd position	Temperance
3rd position	The Chariot
4th position	Seven of Wands (reversed)
5th position	Six of Swords
6th position	Seven of Cups
7th position	Six of Cups
8th position	The Hanged Man (reversed)
9th position	Four of Cups

Reading

Question 1: Do I have spirit guides?

Answer: Five of Swords. This card suggests that Penny does not believe in spirit guides. She desires to overcome others due to her own ego needs and this can lead to rash behavior on her part. Her mental attitude is not positive, and may bring empty victory.

Question 2: How can I contact my spirit guides?

Answer: Temperance. Penny must trust her inner source for guidance and have faith that she will be able to contact her own special guides—meditation is a very good way to do this. Patience is another virtue that Penny must cultivate as she balances her desires with wisdom.

Question 3: Will I make contact with my spirit guides soon?

Answer: The Chariot. This card indicates that now is the time to use one's mental powers to control destiny and be victorious. The charioteer represents Penny's higher self and she must trust it to guide her in all of her affairs. She must have faith that the source is within her and she will soon make contact.

Question 4: Will we communicate only mentally?

Answer: Seven of Wands (reversed). Penny is too focused on her physical and material needs at this time. Her path is unclear and she feels uncertain about her future. She must have more faith and trust in her higher self in order to make any kind of contact—mentally or otherwise.

Question 5: Have my spirit guides been with me always?

Answer: Six of Swords. Penny is not aware of her spirit guides. She is too focused on her problems and troubles and needs more faith in herself. Her higher self is always with her (as with all of us). She must acknowledge this presence within her. Penny has a choice: run away from her problems and troubles or stay and see them through, knowing her higher self and her spirit guides are helping her.

Question 6: Will my guides give me information about my work, home matters, and relationships?

Answer: Seven of Cups. This card indicates that medita-tion and creative visualization will lead Penny to the information she needs. Penny's spirit guides are there to help her through all types of experiences.

Question 7: Can my guides teach me about other realities?

Answer: Six of Cups. Penny has a world of knowledge within herself and her guides can give her this information if she has the ability to accept it. She must make choices about what she wants to know. Penny must be careful not to live in the past or to focus her energies on past relationships.

Question 8: Do spirit guides appear in physical form?

Answer: The Hanged Man (reversed). Penny is easily fooled by others and she should be aware of the risks of living in fantasy or illusion. She does not have faith or trust in a higher power and wants visual proof of its existence. This may not happen, but it does not mean the higher self does not exist.

Question 9: Final outcome?

Answer: Four of Cups. Penny realizes she lives in the past in her relationships. She must overcome depression and become aware that new opportunities await her. Old habit patterns must be discarded, replaced by her realization that she is the one in charge of her life, love, and emotional well-being. Her guides will help with this process, if she lets them.

Comments

Just as we take other things for granted, we must be prepared to accept our inner guidance. Penny needs faith and trust in this concept. As it is said, "When the student is ready, the teacher appears."

SOUL MATE SPREAD

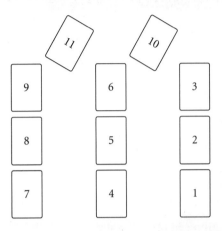

1. How do I contact my soul mate?
2. Is my soul mate in the physical world now?
3. Is it possible to communicate with my soul mate now?
4. What can I do to bring my soul mate into my life?
5. Is my soul mate a free spirit?
6. Have we been in relationships in the past?
7. Do I need to study or learn anything about soul mates?
8. Will there be harmony between us?
9. How can I learn to love and accept my soul mate?
10. What changes can I make while I wait for my soul mate?
11. Final outcome?

Soul Mate Spread for Meredith

Cards in the Spread

1st position	Justice
2nd position	Three of Pentacles
3rd position	Queen of Wands (reversed)
4th position	Four of Pentacles (reversed)
5th position	Three of Cups
6th position	The Sun (reversed)
7th position	Three of Swords
8th position	Four of Cups (reversed)
9th position	Ten of Wands (reversed)
10th position	King of Pentacles (reversed)
11th position	Eight of Wands

Reading

Question 1: How do I contact my soul mate?

Answer: Justice. Meredith can contact her soul mate through acts of kindness, caring, and nurturing others. She must use discrimination in her experiences and treat others as she would like to be treated. Meredith must have faith in her inner source and then she will succeed in contacting her soul mate. Meditation and creative visualization are good ways to do this.

Question 2: Is my soul mate in the physical world now?

Answer: Three of Pentacles. This card refers to the physical world (pentacles), indicating the possibility that Meredith's soul mate is on earth at this time. The Three of Pentacles speaks of a master craftsman, someone who is artistic and good at what he does. He has faith in his abilities and making money through his work. Meredith needs to get busy with her visualization now!

Question 3: Is it possible to communicate with my soul mate now?

Answer: Queen of Wands (reversed). This card reversed depicts a Leo man. Any time Meredith is ready, she can begin to contact her soul mate through meditation and creative visualization. She will be able to make this contact in a matter of weeks if she is persistent!

Question 4: What can I do to bring my soul mate into my life?

Answer: Four of Pentacles (reversed). Meredith's beliefs need to be altered and her thinking directed to positive channels. She may be a spendthrift or a gambler with a need to understand the value of money. She may be involved with negative experiences that she must resolve, or may find herself dealing with health issues.

Question 5: Is my soul mate a free spirit?

Answer: Three of Cups. The answer is yes. This soul mate is happy, has good times, and desires to travel. He is creative and expresses himself through the arts, music, or literature, as well as through his work. Meredith could learn a great deal from her soul mate about enjoying life.

Question 6: Have we been in relationships in the past?

Answer: The Sun (reversed). The Sun card relates to Leo, a sign also seen in Question 3. If there was a past encounter, it was not positive, or perhaps circumstances prevented them from connecting. Reversed, this card speaks of dishonesty, a lack of courage, and low self-esteem. Whether this information relates to Meredith or her soul mate is not clear.

Question 7: Do I need to study or learn anything about soul mates?

Answer: Three of Swords. Meredith may study and learn about anything that interests her, but if her friends are "into" soul mates, she may just be following the crowd. She should recognize that she makes her own problems, and doing spiritual work can raise more issues for her than she realizes. It would be healthy to learn something about "higher knowledge."

Question 8: Will there be harmony between us?

Answer: Four of Cups (reversed). Meredith feels she will be disappointed in this relationship with her soul mate. She is inexperienced in relationships and does not have much faith or trust in other people. There can be harmony and happiness if Meredith will release her negative expectations and be confident that her soul mate cares about her.

Question 9: How can I learn to love and accept my soul mate?

Answer: Ten of Wands (reversed). Meredith must make changes in her life. She feels stagnant both at work and in her social life and is looking for alternatives. She must take responsibility rather than expecting her soul mate to make her world more interesting. Meredith must evaluate her expectations and decide whether she is ready to accept her soul mate unconditionally.

Question 10: What changes can I make while I wait for my soul mate?

Answer: King of Pentacles (reversed). Meredith must overcome some negative traits within herself such as selfishness and being lazy and impractical. She could learn to be more honest, less stubborn, and more loving. Having more faith and trust in herself would also help.

Question 11: Final outcome?

Answer: Eight of Wands. Meredith has the strength to do all of the things suggested by this reading. She can work and have the active social life she seeks, and she can have a healthy relationship with her soul mate. The more positively she thinks, the quicker her soul mate will arrive.

Comments

Meredith must be serious about wanting her soul mate in her life. If she is, she will work on her own issues through meditation and creative visualization. These powerful tools are her keys to success. A few minutes a day, every day, will bring your heart's desire to you. Positive thinking and your beliefs manifest your life.

Soul Mate Spread for Josey

Cards in the Spread

1st position	Two of Pentacles
2nd position	Ace of Cups (reversed)
3rd position	Three of Cups
4th position	Three of Pentacles (reversed)
5th position	Queen of Swords
6th position	Knight of Wands
7th position	The Hermit
8th position	Two of Cups (reversed)
9th position	Ace of Swords
10th position	King of Swords
11th position	Three of Wands

Reading

Question 1: How do I contact my soul mate?

Answer: Two of Pentacles. Josey must learn to balance her physical and material needs with her spiritual values. She must keep herself healthy and have faith in herself. The contact between Josey and her soul mate will occur when she is emotionally balanced.

Question 2: Is my soul mate in the physical world now?

Answer: Ace of Cups (reversed). According to this card, Josey is not receptive to her soul mate at this time. She is emotionally unstable, feels drained, and is quarreling with family members. This is not a time for new beginnings in love or new relationships.

Question 3: Is it possible to communicate with my soul mate now?

Answer: Three of Cups. Communication with Josey's soul mate is possible and it would make her happy to make this contact. Getting involved with her creative side would be beneficial, rather than focusing on her negative experiences with family members.

Question 4: What can I do to bring my soul mate into my life?

Answer: Three of Pentacles (reversed). Josey lacks faith in her abilities. She must be happy, enjoying life, and feeling that life is worthwhile. She must believe that it is possible to encounter her soul mate.

Question 5: Is my soul mate a free spirit?

Answer: Queen of Swords. This Queen is independent, alone, and seeking a relationship. In this position, this card could indicate that Josey's soul mate is a passive, loving, and caring individual, while Josey is more aggressive and independent. Perhaps Josey can learn to temper her aggression and spend more time exploring her feminine side.

Question 6: Have we been in relationships in the past?

Answer: Knight of Wands. This card indicates that Josey and her soul mate have communicated with each other, either in the past or in the present. This would show that they have had a relationship.

Question 7: Do I need to study or learn anything about soul mates?

Answer: The Hermit. Josey must learn to trust and respect herself and then she will be closer to encountering her soul mate. She would be wise to seek her inner teacher for spiritual guidance. Meditation can also help her contact her soul mate.

Question 8: Will there be harmony between us?

Answer: Two of Cups (reversed). Josey knows that she fears commitment and being hurt in love. She is not trusting and this has created emotional problems in her past relationships. If there is no trust in a relationship, there is no need for that relationship, except to learn from it. How can there be harmony or if there is no love or trust?

Question 9: How can I learn to love and accept my soul mate?

Answer: Ace of Swords. Josey must learn to love and accept herself first. Understanding herself is her primary lesson and will change her beliefs. Josey lacks trust, a main ingredient in a relationship. This card can indicate a loss—not a good beginning for a romantic relationship.

Question 10: What changes can I make while I wait for my soul mate?

Answer: King of Swords. Josey must use discrimination in deciding what changes she should make. She must not get too emotionally involved with her family or other relationships. By maintaining her emotional balance and learning to love and respect herself, she can attract her soul mate. She can make these changes by altering her beliefs and becoming aware of her thought patterns.

Question 11: Final outcome?

Answer: Three of Wands. Josey is very creative in her professional and social life. Now she needs to seek inner guidance for future plans that include her soul mate. New ideas will bring success and happiness to Josey if she believes in herself. Creative visualization is a method that Josey could use to change her thinking.

Comments

Josey is a Leo, the sign of the ego. She is very creative and works at a job she loves. She becomes disappointed when her expectations are not met, or when plans do not turn out the way she wants them to. Josey has family problems and relationship issues, but problems are opportunities for growth and we must accept our experiences in a positive manner.

Nine

Just for Fun

In this chapter there are four spreads; three have case studies and the fourth does not. Everyone will love the Wish spread—who does not have millions of wishes? The Magical Lottery spread will be popular and could work out very well for someone who has enough faith.

The spreads are:

Wish
Yes or No
Magical Lottery
Through the Week

The Yes or No spread is self-explanatory and only eight cards are needed. The Through the Week spread utilizes seven cards, one for each day. If you read the spread on Thursday, begin the reading with that day and go through the next week until you have covered seven days. Try them all and see what results you come up with. Have fun!

WISH SPREAD

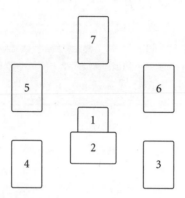

1. What is my wish?
2. Do I feel I deserve my wish?
3. What are the forces opposing my wish?
4. What forces are working for me to help attain my wish?
5. Are there changes I must make to get my wish?
6. Is this wish in my best interests?
7. Outcome?

Wish Spread for Lorna

Cards in the Spread

1st position	Ace of Pentacles (reversed)
2nd position	The Fool
3rd position	The Hanged Man
4th position	Two of Pentacles (reversed)
5th position	The Emperor (reversed)
6th position	Seven of Swords
7th position	The Hierophant (reversed)

Reading

Question 1: What is my wish?

Answer: Ace of Pentacles (reversed). Lorna is concerned about a situation in her neighborhood. Although she is involved in her neighborhood watch program, she is unhappy with the circumstances involved and feels the problem will not go away. Lorna also feels that the property values in the area are affected by the undesirables who roam the streets where she lives. The thought of moving has occurred to her, but this card says "no new beginnings with money," which would make moving into a new area at this time unlikely.

Question 2: Do I feel I deserve my wish?

Answer: The Fool. Lorna's wish is to have others participate as much as she does, but this is a vain hope. She deserves to have support from her neighbors because they are also at risk. Lorna has a full-time job and a fourteen-year-old son at home, which keeps her quite busy.

Question 3: What are the forces opposing my wish?

Answer: The Hanged Man. Lorna feels she must dedicate a lot of time to policing the immediate area and attending meetings, but does not think that others are doing their share. She is sacrificing her will to the desires of others and this is making her ill. Lorna must keep her emotions and her health balanced through meditation and creative visualization.

Question 4: What forces are working for me to help attain my wish?

Answer. Two of Pentacles (reversed). Lorna is depressed because she would like to move, but her financial affairs will not allow her to do so at this time. What she must understand is that she must work out this problem where she is, and not take it with her if she does move. This card indicates a person who does not know how to budget money. Either Lorna is a spendthrift or her husband handles their financial affairs. Money and health balance each other, and we all benefit from this balance.

Question 5: Are there changes I must make to get my wish?

Answer: The Emperor (reversed). Lorna does not realize that she is a good choice for being the leader, authority figure, and spokesperson for her neighborhood. It is natural for most people to let someone else take charge, so Lorna should not let resentment, fear, or immature thinking cloud her vision. Perhaps a meeting and an election would stimulate her neighbors to play a larger role in the watch program.

Question 6: Is this wish in my best interests?

Answer: Seven of Swords. This card refers to problems and troubles that Lorna creates for herself, which are temporary. Her house has been burglarized twice and Lorna feels uncomfortable whenever she is away. Her belief system is attracting her experiences but she is reluctant to accept responsibility for her part in the events. She is capable of being the spokeswoman for the neighborhood watch program, but the choice is hers. Lorna would know what is going on if she continued to work with the group and that would be in her best interests.

Question 7: Outcome?

Answer: The Hierophant (reversed). Lorna does not believe in an inner source. She is a Cancer and desires safety, security, and survival. This is a materialistic view and rarely satisfies the soul. Meditation and creative visualization could be the answer to her prayers, if she would only try.

Comments

Lorna is a school psychologist and, along with her career, she has a husband, a son, and her house to take care of. She is eager to move, although she loves her home. There are four major arcana cards in this spread, which may indicate that four individuals play an important role in Lorna's life at this time. Most of her friends live in a different area—perhaps this factor is the most important clue of all.

Wish Spread for Fred

Cards in the Spread

1st position	Four of Cups
2nd position	Two of Wands
3rd position	The Moon
4th position	Ace of Cups (reversed)
5th position	Three of Cups (reversed)
6th position	Seven of Cups
7th position	Seven of Wands

Reading

Question 1: What is my wish?

Answer: Four of Cups. Fred realizes that he needs to balance his emotions. He is a Scorpio, a water sign, and very intense. Between his business and his family, there is constant turmoil in his life. Looking at the cards in this spread, we see the focus is on love and emotional needs on one hand, and business on the other. He also has a tendency to hang on to past experiences that he should release. Fred's wish is for balance in all areas.

Question 2: Do I feel I deserve my wish?

Answer: Two of Wands. Fred has the world in his hands. He is a successful businessman who understands his work, and his wife and sister are both involved in the business. Fred feels he deserves his good fortune and strives for balance all the time.

Question 3: What are the forces opposing my wish?

Answer: The Moon. On some level, Fred will not face the truth. His wife and sister are in competition for his affections and this is creating problems. Fred might be swayed first one way and then the other by his own emotional needs. He needs to use his intuition to maintain peace and harmony between the two women in his life. The Moon card also refers to Fred's mother. Fred and his sister lost their mother when they were very young. This has created an emotional bond between brother and sister, which would be difficult to break.

Question 4: What forces are working for me to help attain my wish?

Answer: Ace of Cups (reversed). Fred may feel stressed, but he will not have any new beginnings in emotional matters at this time. His business is becoming more and more successful, so there are material forces helping him to victory.

Question 5: Are there changes I must make to get my wish?

Answer: Three of Cups (reversed). This card tells us that Fred does not make himself happy. He is having difficulty in his relationships and it is causing an emotional drain, some depression, and the potential for loss. Perhaps Fred feels lonely due to the problems with his family. The initial change Fred could make is to count his blessings and learn to be satisfied. The women in his life will have to work out their problems of jealousy and resentment without his help.

Question 6: Is this wish in my best interests?

Answer: Seven of Cups. If Fred can maintain his emotional balance, the present problems will ease. His success has brought him material well-being from which his wife and sister naturally benefit. So, while his business has helped everyone materially, it doesn't always help emotionally. Fred has a good imagination and creative visualization has helped him in the past. Daily meditation would help him cope.

Question 7: Outcome?

Answer: Seven of Wands. Fred must take the mental path, which speaks of controlling his emotions. He must rely on his own judgment, but not act egotistically or feel superior.

Comments

Fred has worked very hard for his success and his wife and sister have been instrumental in helping him achieve it. Perhaps it is good that Fred travels a good deal for this business. As long as each person is getting some of his or her ego needs met, conflict is minimized.

Wish Spread for Ken

Cards in the Spread

1st position	Three of Pentacles
2nd position	Ten of Cups
3rd position	Queen of Swords (reversed)
4th position	Page of Cups (reversed)
5th position	Page of Pentacles (reversed)
6th position	Five of Wands (reversed)
7th position	Page of Wands

Reading

Question 1: What is my wish?

Answer: Three of Pentacles. Ken is a lawyer. He feels he is a master craftsman who makes money because he is good at what he does. Ken's wish is to remain productive and take care of his family's needs and his own.

Question 2: Do I feel I deserve my wish?

Answer: Ten of Cups. Ken feels strongly that he deserves to get his wish. He has recently married for a second time and started a new family. His children from his first marriage are all adults and able to take care of their own needs.

Question 3: What are the forces opposing my wish?

Answer: Queen of Swords (reversed). This Queen has problems and troubles but may not wish to confront them. She has been married but is now divorced. This card represents Ken's sister who does not care for Ken's new wife and tries to create trouble between them. Ken tries to maintain peace between these two women and is not always successful. There is a certain amount of jealousy involved as Ken's new wife is much younger than Ken. Fortunately, Ken knows his sister well and understands that she is a manipulator.

Question 4: What forces are working for me to help attain my wish?

Answer: Page of Cups (reversed). This Page symbolizes an emotional drain and many disappointments but also great expectations. Ken has three children from his first marriage and his son was constantly in trouble. Now Ken has a second son who is very young and lovable. This boy may be the force that is working for Ken to help him attain his wish.

Question 5: Are there changes I must make to get my wish?

Answer: Page of Pentacles (reversed). This Page is not interested in getting an education, setting goals, or learning how to earn money to be independent. This could refer to the older son who wants the easy life, dislikes authority, and has been involved with drugs. Perhaps he feels rejected by Ken since he was young when his parents divorced. The changes that Ken needs to make concern this son. Showing him unconditional love may help the young man and also help Ken to get his wish.

Question 6: Is this wish in my best interests?

Answer: Five of Wands (reversed). Ken feels that he has been very fortunate in his life, but he is afraid that his relationship will not remain as happy as it has been. His wish for financial success is positive and by affirming prosperity, his circumstances should not change. Ken's health has also been good and by keeping a positive outlook, it should remain so.

Question 7: Outcome?

Answer: Page of Wands. This Page is headstrong, desires freedom, is eager for new experiences, and is independent. Ken said this described one of his daughters, of whom he is very proud. His other daughter has turned out fine, as well. Ken realizes he has another chance with his young son and hopes to do a better job this time.

Comments

It is difficult to start a new family when the parent is in his fifties. Ken loves all of his children, but was not always there for the older ones. When parents and children have high expectations for each other, it is a set-up for disappointment. All a person can do is try to do the best that he can, which Ken feels he is doing.

YES OR NO

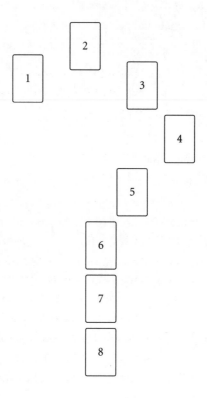

1. What is the question?
2. How is it affecting me?
3. What are the obstacles to overcome?
4. What are my past experiences regarding the question?
5. What are my present thoughts regarding the question?
6. What will occur in the future?
7. Will I need professional advice?
8. Outcome?

Yes or No for Polly

Cards in the Spread

1st position	Nine of Cups
2nd position	Five of Wands
3rd position	The Hierophant (reversed)
4th position	The Wheel of Fortune (reversed)
5th position	Four of Swords
6th position	Seven of Pentacles
7th position	Queen of Wands
8th position	The High Priestess

Reading

Question 1: What is the question?

Answer: Nine of Cups. This is the "wish card" and it is upright, which indicates Polly will get her wish. Polly's question pertains to going into partnership with a friend. Polly has tried several times to work with female partners but has never been successful. She realizes this problem stems from her relationship with her mother. Polly thinks she needs to find a man to partner with, and even that may not work out.

Question 2: How is it affecting me?

Answer: Five of Wands. Polly and her friend each want their own way in this venture. They each believe they know the best way to do things at work, but their ego needs are creating a power struggle. Polly is constantly finding fault with her friend, which is not a good sign.

Question 3: What are the obstacles to overcome?

Answer. The Hierophant (reversed). Polly does not wish to follow any rules or regulations in her venture. She is a rebel who desires to do things her way, and could be putting stumbling blocks in her own path with this attitude. Polly wants to control all aspects of the business, so having a partner may not be the best answer.

Question 4: What are my past experiences regarding the question?

Answer: The Wheel of Fortune (reversed). Polly should not gamble or take chances with her venture. In the past, she had partners and felt they all took advantage of her. She still believes that she will attract someone who will do the same thing to her now. With this belief, she should not get involved with a partner of any kind.

Question 5: What are my present thoughts regarding the question?

Answer: Four of Swords. Polly should rest and meditate on her problems. She needs to balance her emotions and recognize that she is creating her own experiences through her uncontrolled ego and immature attitude.

Question 6: What will occur in the future?

Answer: Seven of Pentacles. This card shows that Polly can have money and will have to make decisions about what to do with it. The money may come suddenly and she needs to be prepared. This is a hopeful sign for her business venture.

Question 7: Will I need professional advice?

Answer: Queen of Wands. Polly wants to do it all herself, but she must seek legal counsel for her new venture if she wants to protect herself and her product. This card symbolizes the ego in work and social life. Polly wants to be a star, and be admired and praised. If this card represents the partner, however, Polly must proceed with caution.

Question 8: Outcome?

Answer: The High Priestess. The High Priestess says, "I know." This card indicates that Polly has the answer to her question within her. She is intelligent and if she does not let her need for money or her ego get in the way, success is assured.

Comments

Polly would like to change her occupation. Her new venture looks promising and could make her a winner, but she must follow legal procedure, even if she is a rebel. The future looks bright for her.

Yes or No for Darla

Cards in the Spread

1st position	Four of Pentacles (reversed)
2nd position	Eight of Pentacles (reversed)
3rd position	The Chariot (reversed)
4th position	Five of Pentacles
5th position	Seven of Cups (reversed)
6th position	Ten of Pentacles (reversed)
7th position	Six of Swords (reversed)
8th position	Justice

Reading

Question 1: What is the question?

Answer: Four of Pentacles (reversed). There is a lack of balance in Darla's mental attitude. Her thinking is materially based, and her sense of money is also out of balance, although she is not greedy. Her question concerned her job as a teacher, and whether she would still be working at the same school when the next semester starts.

Question 2: How is it affecting me?

Answer: Eight of Pentacles (reversed). Darla feels she is working with dishonest people and she senses a lack of strength within herself to deal with them. Health problems can arise if she feels powerless, but Darla is a strong Scorpio and very capable of holding her own in most situations.

Question 3: What are the obstacles to overcome?

Answer: The Chariot (reversed). Darla may feel she is not in control of her desires or her finances. She does not feel secure or nurtured at this time, and is not in touch with her inner source, which is there to guide her.

Question 4: What are my past experiences regarding the question?

Answer: Five of Pentacles. Darla used to focus too much on money and made it her god. This is a crippling belief, but fortunately she learned through experience that it is not healthy and put it behind her. Darla is good at what she does and need not fear losing her job.

Question 5: What are my present thoughts regarding the question?

Answer: Seven of Cups (reversed). Darla is emotionally drained due to a conflict that took place at work. Perhaps if Darla were to creatively visualize herself starting the new semester in September, she would feel more secure and assured about her job.

Question 6: What will occur in the future?

Answer: Ten of Pentacles (reversed). There are no changes ahead for Darla's finances. She is working and understands that she must cut back on her expenses and pay off her debts. This could take some pressure off and prevent worries in the future.

Question 7: Will I need professional advice?

Answer: Six of Swords (reversed). Darla is not making choices right now, but she must stay and face her troubles. She must also use her mind to analyze her problems and not allow others to make decisions for her.

Question 8: Outcome?

Answer: Justice. Darla may need legal advice to resolve the situation, or to ensure that she is treated fairly. If there is a legal suit, it is likely she would win.

Comments

Darla has four pentacle cards in her spread, which shows money is a prime factor in her life. She also has many reversed cards. These are not all negative, but to have so many in a spread is significant. Darla must change some of her beliefs in order to change her life. Meditation helps to root out negative beliefs and habit patterns and Darla would benefit greatly from this.

MAGICAL LOTTERY SPREAD

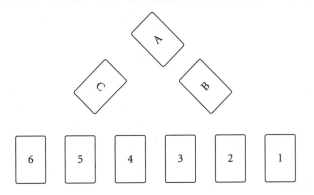

A. Is this a good day to buy a ticket in the lottery?

B. What obstacles must be overcome?

C. What is my attitude toward winning the lottery?

1 through 6: These cards will provide the numbers to play in the lottery.

To Use This Spread

For this spread, you will use only the twenty-two major arcana cards. After you have separated them from the rest of the deck, shuffle the cards. Place one card face up in the A position, another on B, and a third on C. If a card falls in a reversed position, read it that way. If the cards are negative, end the reading at this point and try another day. If the cards are positive, continue with the reading.

Next, place three cards in each position, 1 through 6, face up. These are the lottery numbers. One card will remain; this will be read at the end of the session. After you have read the A, B, and C cards, you are ready to start on position 1. Pick up the three cards in this position and add the numbers of the cards together. Do not reduce the number values of any cards. If the total is over the limit of the lottery, stop the reading and try another day.

Example: Suppose position 1 contains the Moon, the Hierophant, and Justice.

The Moon	18
The Hierophant	5
Justice	11
	34

The amount of this box would be thirty-four, which is within the number range of the lottery. Pick up the three cards in position 2 and add them in the same way. Repeat this with the rest of the boxes, adding each box separately. When you are finished, there will be a total for each of the six boxes. Next, turn over the last card to get the final message.

The application of the final card is up to you. If it is a low-numbered card—The Magician (1) or The High Priestess (2)—you may wish to substitute it for one of the six numbers gained through adding the major arcana cards in the six piles of the reading. Because you have added the values of the numbers in these piles, it is impossible to play a one or two in the lottery simply using those numbers.

If the totals in each of the six positions are within lottery limits, go buy a ticket. Do not wait for another day—do it now!

Remember, when the cards are in the positions numbered 1 through 6, it doesn't matter if they are upright or reversed. When the cards are in positions A, B, and C, they must be read the way they are found—upright or reversed.

Magical Lottery for Arlene

Cards in the Spread

A	The Devil (reversed)	
B	The Sun (reversed)	
C	The Fool (reversed)	
Position 1	The Wheel of Fortune	10
	Death	13
	The High Priestess	2
Position 2	The Tower	16
	Judgement	20
	The Chariot	7
Position 3	The Magician	1
	The Hierophant	5
	The World	21
Position 4	The Hanged Man	12
	The Empress	3
	The Emperor	4
Position 5	The Lovers	6
	Temperance	14
	The Moon	18
Position 6	The Hermit	9
	The Star	17
	Justice	11
Last card	Strength	8

Reading:

Question 1: Is this a good day to buy a ticket in the lottery?

Answer: The Devil (reversed). Arlene is not as greedy for material possessions or as selfish as she could be, but there is a block in her thinking that refuses to allow her to have abundance in her life.

Question 2: What obstacles must be overcome?

Answer: The Sun (reversed). Arlene has a lack of courage or confidence. She must learn to be open and honest with others, which builds trust and respect. Arlene places too much emphasis on the physical or sexual side of her life. This is the time to overcome past beliefs and habit patterns and learn to love oneself.

Question 3: What is my attitude toward winning the lottery?

Answer: The Fool (reversed). Arlene's attitudes and beliefs are sabotaging her desires. She must balance her actions and her emotions, and learn to have faith in herself. If Arlene does not feel she deserves to win the lottery, she never will.

Position 1 Total—25

Position 2 Total—43

Position 3 Total—27

Position 4 Total—19

Position 5 Total—38

Position 6 Total—37

Because the final card of Arlene's reading was Strength, with a numerological value of eight, the number was disregarded and she played the six numbers she was given. It does, however, indicate that she has the strength to overcome all obstacles and change her life for the better.

Arlene's reading was done on Thursday and she bought a ticket on Saturday. She did not win anything—this time.

Comments

Buy a ticket on the day you put out a positive spread. Good luck!

THROUGH THE WEEK

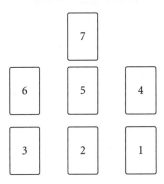

1. What new plans can I make for this day?
2. Will my plans include another person?
3. Will I enjoy this day?
4. Will I do good work today and be productive?
5. What changes or new experiences will I encounter today?
6. What new responsibilities or family issues will I be involved with today?
7. Will this be a day of rest or mental activity?